# Inspiring Quality In Your School

*From Theory to Practice*

ROBERT A. SULLO

## ADVISORY PANEL

Neil Chivington
School Counselor/Social Worker
Buxton, Maine

Marian Trainor
Former Elementary Teacher
Media Specialist
Warren Consolidated Schools
Lomphere Schools

Mozella Locklear
Alamance-Burlington—Retired

Evelyn Johnson Mims
Retired English, Speech and
Drama Teacher,
Tuscaloosa City School
Tuscaloosa, Alabama

Vanessa S. Baugh
School Counselor
Penn-Trafford School District

Jack Bradford
Mathematics Teacher
Flathead High School
Kalispell, Montana

John J. Tzeng
U.S. Department of State
(former professor of media/library
and instructional systems,
University of the District of Columbia)

Copyright © 1997 National Education Association of the United States

Printing History
    First Printing: June 1997

This book is printed on acid-free paper.          This book is printed with soy ink.

**Library of Congress Cataloging-in-Publication Data**

Sullo, Robert A., 1951-
Inspiring quality in your school: from theory to practice/by Robert A. Sullo.
p. cm. — (The Inspired classroom series)
Includes bibliographical references.
ISBN 0-8106-2951-8 (pbk.)

1. School improvement programs—United States. 2. School management and organization—United States. 3. Quality control—United States. 4. Effective teaching—United States. 5. Educational change—United States. I. Title. II. Series.
LB2822.82.S85   1997
371.2'00973—dc21                                             97–15029
                                                                                CIP

*This book is for the thousands of teachers who inspire quality in classrooms around the world. Each day you help students discover that learning truly adds quality to their lives.*

# Contents

# *Introduction*

This book is written both for my colleagues in education and everyone considering a career in education. When I began writing, I anticipated this would be almost exclusively professional in nature and in focus. It became clear early on, however, that I was not interested in separating the personal from the professional. I began to think about what I say and do in workshops with teachers across the country as I teach the concepts of choice theory, reality therapy, and quality schools. I quickly discovered that a major theme in my presentations and discussions is the integration of these concepts into our personal lives. In fact, I'm convinced that it is virtually impossible to regularly behave in a way consistent with the principles of choice theory, reality therapy, and quality schools in a professional setting without putting these same concepts to work in our personal lives as well. That's not to say you can't utilize these concepts at all if you don't integrate them in your personal life. In my experience, however, people who are true quality teachers behave in ways that are congruent with these concepts at home and in the world at large, as well as in the classroom. Those who limit their application of choice theory and reality therapy ideas to a professional setting are almost never as effective or satisfied, personally or professionally.

Integrating the personal and the professional adds value to my presentations. To separate the two here seems like leaving out the essence of what I believe. The integrated person celebrates life by bringing quality to everything they experience.

*Inspiring Quality in Your School* is built upon the notion that meaningful change occurs from the inside out. If we want to add quality to our profession and our professional lives, we must begin where we have the most influence: with ourselves.

## IMPROVING SCHOOLS

As a faculty member of The William Glasser Institute, I have the opportunity to meet and work with teachers from around the country. Teachers have always been interested in improving education. *The Quality School*, published by Dr. Glasser in 1990, provides a focus and context for many discussions designed to improve our schools.

Everywhere I go, teachers face similar challenges. Our triumphs and frustrations are remarkably alike. Some of us work in small schools and some in large; some of us work in urban schools and some in rural; some of us work with elementary age children and some with high schoolers. Despite our many differences, we all work with children and we all want to do the best job we can.

I have spent 23 years in public education, both as a classroom teacher and a school psychologist. This is a challenging time for those of us who have decided to dedicate our professional lives to public education. We are easy targets for the malcontents of society and are, therefore, attacked regularly. By the same token, these are exciting times in education. As the public clamors for educational reform, we have an opportunity to actively involve ourselves in the creation of schools that are even better than the ones we have today. In many ways, the choice is ours. We can sit back idly and let others define what role we will play or we can share our insights and visions about how to make our public schools truly exciting learning laboratories.

This book is based upon my experiences as a public school educator with a strong belief in the principles of choice theory and reality therapy. While it is fashionable to talk about quality in education, such discussions often seem trivial or superficial. Everyone is in favor of quality education. The key is to raise the discussion to a level that brings it above the superficial. We need to find a way to make the concepts of quality and quality schools specific enough so that professionals can put these notions to work in their day-to-day interactions with students.

## OBJECTIVES OF THIS BOOK

I have built *Inspiring Quality In Your School* upon several key premises.

- **Premise #1:** If you don't know where you want to go, it's hard to know if you're on the right road.

- **Premise #2:** One of the best ways to teach something is to model it.

- **Premise #3:** The more we discuss, process, define, and argue about issues that matter, the more we will learn and grow in positive directions.

The primary objective of this book is to offer teachers and prospective teachers some ideas about quality and some notions about how you can apply these ideas, both personally and in your chosen profession. These are my opinions and are given only for you to consider. There may be circumstances that I have not experienced or have neglected to consider as I attempt to capture how to create quality. One of my strengths, however, is that I have very little need to be "right" or to have "the final word" about what makes a quality school. What I want is for us to make continual progress on our journey to quality. It is enough for me to help move the discussion along. If where we end up is different from where I initially envision, that's fine with me. I have faith that we will be moving in the right direction as long as we keep the discussions focused and honest. I merely offer my thoughts for you to consider, discuss, and improve upon.

What contribution do I want to make to the field of education? I want to help initiate further dialogue about how to develop quality schools. While I want to be able to contribute some of the "answer," it is more important for me to help create an environment where as many teachers as possible become involved in collectively creating the quality schools where they work. As I considered my goal, I decided that writing this book offers me the best chance at this time to make a meaningful contribution to our field.

## HOW THIS BOOK IS ORGANIZED

**Part I** provides an overview of choice theory, reality therapy, and quality schools. This theoretical foundation is necessary if we are to build strategies upon a coherent and integrated foundation.

**Part II** incorporates concepts aimed at the individual as well as the school as a whole and offers an opportunity for practitioners to begin to apply the concepts introduced in Part I.

**Part III** provides a discussion of some of the topics teachers will most likely want to consider when they build their own quality school. Topics covered include:

- homework
- tests
- grading
- grade retention
- ability grouping
- co-teaching
- discipline/management.

You will find much to think about as you read the following pages. I hope that you agree more than disagree with what is offered. More important, I ask you to reflect upon what you encounter and to share your ideas with your colleagues. The more who are involved in our discussions about quality, the easier our journey will be.

There is creative reading as well as creative writing. Bring forth your creativity as you read and as you work with your colleagues to build an even better school.

# PART I

# *Inspiring Quality— Theory*

# CHAPTER 1

# *Whose Life Is It Anyway ?*

Before beginning any formal discussion of choice theory or reality therapy, I want to tell you why I think these ideas are so important and why I believe in these principles so strongly. One of the key concepts in choice theory and reality therapy is the notion of personal responsibility. It is also a cognitive approach to getting people to reflect upon and evaluate their behaviors. Many who work with young children and are unfamiliar with reality therapy become concerned that the approach is "beyond" the ability level of the children they serve, that it is developmentally inappropriate. "This may be fine with adolescents and adults," they say, "but I would never be able to use it in my second grade classroom."

I offer you the following two stories and ask you to think about both the concept of responsibility and the capacity of young children to reflect upon and evaluate their own behaviors. Seemingly unrelated, the stories capture the difference between seeing the world through a choice theory lens and seeing the world from a more traditional viewpoint.

Choice theory was originally called "control theory." In 1996, Dr. Glasser decided to have this theory of human behavior identified as "choice theory." This name more accurately reflects a central belief in this framework: that we forever choose how to behave as we live our lives. I have found that an understanding and application of choice theory principles helps us claim responsibility for our own lives and celebrate this essential aspect of our humanity. The following two stories illustrate what I mean.

## KAREN'S STORY

Karen is a colleague with whom I have worked for over twenty years. Her dedication to the field of education and to students is remarkable. To put it simply, I would be delighted if Karen were my child's teacher. She runs a classroom that involves a lot of laughter, joy, hard work, and skill building. Students leave her class much more competent than when they enter and they enjoy themselves along the way. This does not mean there are no upsets or difficulties in her classroom, but these are viewed by Karen as opportunities for her and her students to grow and develop even greater competence. When all is said and done, students in Karen's classroom become more responsible, more skilled, and better educated.

Several years ago, I noticed that she seemed less energetic and joyful than usual. One morning, just before the 1900-plus students in our school were about to enter the building, I asked how things were going and mentioned I had sensed that she was less "up" than usual. Her comments were particularly revealing, I thought. While she indicated that there were certain current stresses that might be temporarily draining, Karen quickly added, "But the bell is about to ring and soon the corridors will be filled with kids. Then my energy will return. It's almost magical. Once I see the kids, I feel so much better. It just happens to me and I have no control over it. They make my day!"

Over the years, Karen has expressed an interest in choice theory and reality therapy and has done some reading in this area. In the few minutes that we had together that morning, I asked if she were able to accept that the good feelings she experienced when she saw the students didn't "just happen," wasn't "magical," but was related to choices she makes regularly as a dedicated teacher. In that brief interaction, I was trying to help Karen take responsibility for her success. Despite our involvement over a period of years, Karen ended our conversation with the comment, "I know. That's your reality therapy stuff. I'd rather see it as just magic."

## MELANIE'S STORY

My daughter Melanie was seven years old and in the second grade when the following incident occurred.

Melanie was invited to participate in a group piano lesson. Generally, Melanie has private lessons. While she enjoys playing for family members, Melanie is not particularly comfortable playing in front of others until she feels competent with whatever is going to be played. Several days before the group lesson, my wife told me that Melanie seemed concerned about the upcoming lesson and asked me if I would speak with her about it. My conversation with Melanie represents one of the most joyful moments of my parenting experience.

I began by simply asking Melanie, "So what's the story with this lesson?" She looked at me and with perfect innocence, clarity, and focus answered, "Dad, I really don't know. There's just something in my head and I'm choosing to be nervous about this." Choosing to be nervous! I didn't know whether to laugh or cry tears of joy. Here was a seven-year old girl taking total responsibility for her feelings and her life, even an unpleasant aspect. Her innocence as she behaved in such a responsible, fully human way was almost comical. Simultaneously, I could feel the tears well up within me as I witnessed my daughter confronting her life and taking full responsibility. It was truly a quality moment.

I then asked Melanie if she would prefer to choose something other than nervousness as she prepared for her lesson. "Of course,"she said; she just didn't know what else she could do. After I reminded her that one of my roles as a parent is to help her when she gets stuck, we had a three minute conversation and came up with some alternatives. We agreed to speak again the next evening after dinner to review if things improved.

Melanie has learned, at her young age, that she controls her own life. While that does not mean that things, both good and bad, don't happen "to" her, it does mean that she controls her life much more fully than most people believe they can. That knowledge will help her live her life in the fullest possible way.

## CHOICE THEORY AND ME

For me, choice theory is more than a theory of human behavior and motivation. It is part of a belief system that allows me to embrace my humanity completely. It challenges me every step of the way but it offers me the ultimate satisfaction of living the responsible life, owning my feelings, my sorrows and joys, and claiming my humanity. As these stories illustrate, age, dedication, and cognitive ability all have little to do with the application of choice theory ideas.

Whose life is it, anyway? Karen's story suggests that she does not own her feeling of elation and joy when she sees the kids she cares so much about. She believes it "just happens to her," that she has "no control over it." She fails to take responsibility for her success. It doesn't mean that Karen is not a wonderful teacher. It does mean, however, that Karen sees the world in a way that separates her feelings from her actions. It's a world view that can be dehumanizing and deadening.

Melanie's story is a celebration of life. She assumed ownership of her uncomfortable feelings. As I continue to learn from her, I watch this child raised in a home where we practice choice theory principles to the best of our abilities, and I see her assume responsibility for her many successes as well. She is fully alive, and that is one reason why it is such a pleasure to be in her presence.

As I continue to teach choice theory, it is no longer enough for me to assume an exclusively cognitive, detached posture as I discuss why these ideas are important. Living according to choice theory principles involves a fundamental shift for many people, especially adults. Choice theory is more than taking effective control of your life. It represents a life of total responsibility and gives us an opportunity to embrace what it means to be fully human. With this spirit, I invite you to read, reflect, and evaluate.

# CHAPTER 2

# Choice Theory

## WHY BEGIN WITH THEORY?

Teachers, like many others, are busy, pragmatic people. Not surprisingly, they want to "cut to the chase" as quickly as possible. We live in a culture that looks for quick answers and wants to get through the preliminaries with as little time "wasted" as possible. Many would rather jump immediately to a discussion of a quality school and skip any discussion about theory. Here's a fair question: "Why is it necessary to talk about theory at all?"

I choose to highlight the theoretical. My two reasons for this are:

1. Practice built upon a strong theory will endure.

2. Practice without a strong, articulated, and internalized theory to support it, will almost assuredly fail.

## A Strong Foundation Gives You Strength

Just as a house must be supported by a strong foundation, a quality school must be supported by a strong theoretical foundation: choice theory.

What is the value in being well versed in any theory? Can't practice stand alone? No. Before too long, you will encounter something that isn't covered in even the most comprehensive catalogue of strategies. At that point, you will be better off if you have a strong theoretical base that can provide you with direction so you can creatively face a new challenge. Specific strategies only offer you a cookbook approach to education. Intimate knowledge of a theory allows you to evolve into a master chef who can create a recipe for success.

A theory is a model of how something operates. It provides a framework for understanding a given system so that you can work with that system with relative ease. Being grounded in a theory means that you don't have to get bogged down with every detail.

## Learning Theory Is an Investment

Learning a theory is not unlike making any investment. Think about the investment you made by getting a college education. Some of your classmates from high school made different choices, immediately joining the world of work. They started earning money right away while many of us spent four years or more compiling a financial debt. While there are exceptions, statistics suggest that over a period of time those of us who invested in a college education will be financially better off. Even in a field like education, which does not pay nearly as well as many other professions, we are generally better off financially after investing in our education.

Learning a theory will take some time. It will take even longer to integrate it into your personal and professional lives ("Walking the walk" and not just "talking the talk"). Your colleagues who choose to master strategies and practices without the support of theory will be like those who choose not to invest in a college education. They will appear better off at first; in fact, it might be fair to say that they *are* better off at first. But being a professional in the field of education is much more like a marathon than a 100 yard dash. The most successful are those who invest wisely. That's one benefit of mastering a theory.

*NOTE: If you choose to skip ahead to* Part II Inspiring Quality—Practice *promise yourself, here and now, that if you find the strategies presented helpful, you will return to this part and "invest wisely" in the theory.*

# THE ORIGINS OF CHOICE THEORY

Choice theory is a theory of human behavior that explains how and why we behave the way we do. The development and application of choice theory principles has been one of the major contributions of William Glasser, founder and president of the William Glasser Institute. Dr. Glasser, along with many others, has written extensively about choice theory and its application in a variety of settings. Those interested in reading more are urged to consult the list of suggested readings at the end of this book.

Choice theory is certainly not the only theory explaining human behavior. In fact, it is less well known than stimulus-response psychology, currently the most widely-known theory of human behavior, at least in North America. Perhaps the easiest way for me to explain what choice theory is, especially to an audience of educators and future educators, is to discuss it with reference to stimulus-response psychology. Nearly every professional educator has had some training in stimulus-response psychology. Some educators are highly trained in that area and know the theory and its accompanying practices and strategies well. It is often helpful to introduce something relatively new by referencing something familiar.

### Stimulus-Response Psychology

I will give only a relatively brief overview of stimulus-response psychology since my intention is to explain choice theory. A comparison of the two theories, or models of understanding human behavior, is worthwhile and can promote interesting dialogue. Stimulus-response psychology teaches us:

- when we observe a behavior that we wish to increase in frequency, we should reward or reinforce that behavior.

- when we observe a behavior that we wish to eliminate or decrease in frequency, we should punish the behavior. The punishment may be as mild as ignoring the behavior or may become as intrusive as employing physical force.

Stimulus-response theorists and practitioners would always prefer to use positive reinforcement rather than punishment. Many current practitioners eliminate virtually all references to punishment. Stimulus-response advocates are as sensitive and caring as any other group. Their theory, however, is based upon the premise that people are externally controlled. Through rewards and punishments, our behavior is shaped by external forces. The rewards and punishments may occur randomly or be presented systematically. Stimulus-response advocates suggest that we systematically develop a system of rewards that will shape the behavior we want. While there is nothing sinister in that, the fact remains that the foundation upon which stimulus-response psychology is built is a belief in the external control of human behavior.

Choice theory psychology is based upon the belief that people are internally, not externally, motivated. What drives our behavior are powerful instructions that are built into our genetic structure. The outside world, including all rewards and punishments, only provides us with information. It does not control us or *make* us do anything.

From a foundation perspective, stimulus-response psychology and choice theory psychology are as far apart as any two theories can be that attempt to explain human behavior. Put simply, they cannot both be right. People cannot be *both* internally *and* externally motivated.

Because most of us have had some training in stimulus-response psychology, many of us accept this theory as "truth" without giving it a great deal of thought. What follows provides you with an opportunity to take a closer look at stimulus-response psychology and its implications. I invite you to think about these issues more seriously than you ever have before.

■ **A CLOSER LOOK AT S-R PSYCHOLOGY** Stimulus-response psychology is essentially a mechanistic approach to understanding human behavior. It takes the position that our actions are determined by outside events.

In operant conditioning, the major application of the stimulus-response model, our behavior is seen as a response to rewards and punishments. The practice of behavior modification is based upon operant conditioning principles and suggests that we can control the behavior of others through the systematic administration of rewards and punishments. While a complete behavior modification model is complex and multifaceted, it is based upon a relatively simple stimulus-response principle: rewarded behaviors will increase in frequency and punished behaviors will decrease in frequency. The system and type of rewards and punishments will, of course, vary to fit specific circumstances, but the underlying belief that behavior is a controllable response to rewards and punishments remains constant.

Initially, stimulus-response psychology was greeted with enthusiasm. People were excited by the limitless possibilities suggested by John Watson (1925), the founder of behaviorism, when he wrote:

Give me a dozen healthy infants, well formed, and my own specific world to bring them up in and I'll guarantee to take any one at random and train him to become any kind of specialist I might select—doctor, lawyer, artist, merchant-chief and yes, even beggarman and thief, regardless of his talents, penchants, tendencies, abilities, vocations, and race of his ancestors.

While Watson's bold claims were largely unsubstantiated, the quest to systematically shape "perfect" people remained strong and stimulus-response ideas continued to flourish.

■ **IS FREEDOM AN ILLUSION?** More recently, behaviorism has become most strongly linked to B.F. Skinner, commonly viewed as the most influential psychologist of 20th century America. Skinner painted a picture of a "utopian" society in *Walden Two* (Macmillan, 1948), suggesting that heavenly bliss is available to us here and now if we faithfully implement the principles of operant conditioning.

A belief in Skinner's system of operant conditioning, however, is not without consequence. Skinner emphatically stated on numerous occasions that freedom is an illusion. For those of us who value living in a democratic society, one based upon the notion of free choice, Skinner's assertion deserves to be examined closely and carefully.

- Do we subscribe to and propagate a theory of human behavior that is contrary to the notion of personal freedom?

- Can we accept a view of humanity that reduces us to reactive creatures, equally capable of being programmed through the systematic administration of rewards and punishment as any computer or robot?

- If we agree with Skinner that freedom is an illusion, then what becomes of our concept of what it means to be human?

For too long, these fundamental questions have been essentially brushed aside while the ideas of operant conditioning continue to be advanced in virtually every major university and have permeated our basic social structures, including our families and our schools.

■ **THE ISSUE OF RESPONSIBILITY** While the concept of responsibility has always been part of our democratic social structure, the term is used with increasing frequency, both in schools and society at large. Managers devise systems of accountability. Schools and parents stress personal responsibility. Those who believe in the principles of stimulus-response psychology must find themselves in an uncomfortable position, however, for how can we hold people responsible for their actions if they are nothing more than reactive creatures whose behavior has been determined by outside events? I can only be held responsible for my actions if I am free, if my behavior truly represents a choice I have made. It is a philosophical contradiction of enormous proportions to hold the beliefs that:

1. freedom is an illusion and

2. people are responsible for their behavior.

Yet, a majority of people in our society continue to champion these contradictory positions.

One of the unintentional but significant by-products of a belief in stimulus-response psychology is an increase in irresponsibility. At first such a comment may seem difficult to fathom. With its systematic use of rewards and punishments, stimulus-response psychology claims to promote the development of responsibility. Unfortunately, it does not. People raised by parents and educators practicing rewards and punishment come to see themselves as passive reactors— people whose success or failure is largely attributable to people and things outside of themselves. Such an attitude is as pervasive among successful people as among less successful ones. Many simply view their success as something that "happened" to them. (Remember Karen in the story at the beginning of Part I?) Excuse-making and irresponsibility is rampant among less successful people who blame spouses, parents, children, the government, and society for their troubles.

How is behavior modification and stimulus-response psychology implicated in this failure to accept personal responsibility? Over time, people who are raised with the message that their behavior is controlled from the outside incorporate that orientation into their personality. Children who are told that their parents "make" them behave, who are told that their teachers "make" them do their homework and "make" them learn their lessons, often develop a belief system that they are "made" by outside forces. Such children frequently become quite adept at excuse-making and externalizing, blaming teachers and parents for their failures at school and at home, blaming friends for breakdowns in relationships, blaming other, outside sources for a host of irresponsible behaviors.

The adoption of a position of irresponsibility should not surprise us when many of us have told our children that we would "make" them behave, do their homework, clean their rooms, etc. Our reliance on the principles of stimulus-response psychology has unwittingly fostered the creation of a society alarmingly unwilling to accept personal responsibility and to appreciate that our success and happiness is largely a product of our own choices, freely made.

Stimulus-response psychology, along with all of its manifestations such as behavior modification, is flawed. Time and time again human beings demonstrate that we are more than reactive beings programmed by rewards and punishments and subject to the control of outside influences. Our behavior, in fact, is motivated by powerful genetic instructions, by universal psychological needs that are internal, not external. Choice theory psychology, a new, very different way to understand human motivation and behavior, allows us to reclaim our humanity. With a thorough knowledge of choice theory, we begin to see that we are, in fact, free and can reasonably expect people to behave responsibly. Living in such a world represents a substantial challenge, but it is an exciting one that provides dignity to us as human beings.

## Choice Theory and The Basic Needs

Choice theory is a biological theory that suggests that all of our behavior is internally motivated. We are born with certain specific needs, both physical and psychological, and we have been genetically programmed to behave in an attempt to satisfy these needs. All of our behavior can be understood as our best attempt at any given moment to satisfy our basic needs or genetic instructions. In addition to the well-established and accepted physical needs related to survival (hunger, thirst, warmth, etc.), we have basic psychological needs that must be satisfied if we are to be emotionally healthy.

The four basic psychological needs identified in choice theory are:

- love or belonging,
- power or competence,
- freedom, and
- fun.

While not all of our behavior is responsible or effective, it always represents our best attempt to satisfy one or more of our basic needs. Choice theory teaches us that when people have better, more effective behaviors available to them to satisfy their needs, they will give up less responsible, less effective behaviors. Our goal then, as parents and educators, is to help children develop effective and appropriate behavioral choices as they try continuously to satisfy their basic psychological needs.

At this point, let's look at each of the basic psychological needs identified by choice theory.

■ **LOVE/BELONGING** The need for love/belonging is what drives most of us to live in groups. The need to belong explains why we are social beings. This instruction leads us to cooperate with others. Millions of years ago, those primitive people who developed the ability to cooperate, and stayed together were able to survive and thrive. Over time, through the process of natural selection, the instruction to be loving became part of what it means to be human.

Think of everyone you know. They all have *some* particularly close, valued relationships. Even those who might describe themselves as less social have some especially strong and intimate relationships. Despite the fact that choice theory celebrates our individuality and uniqueness, almost all of us enjoy connecting with others and being part of some larger system. The need to belong is what leads us to join teams, groups, and civic organizations. Without the need for love and belonging, we would only be able to be independent. This social, cooperative instruction allows us to transcend independence and move toward interdependence where we can experience greater quality.

Driven by our genetic instruction to connect with others, we naturally seek ways to belong to a group. Classrooms and schools can be places where teachers and students alike find they can follow this instruction in a responsible and growth-producing way. If we fail to make our school a place where this need can be met responsibly and in a healthy way, our students will be driven to look elsewhere.

■ **POWER** Power is perhaps the most misunderstood of the basic needs because we often think of power in an exclusively competitive sense, identifying it as power over other people. In fact, power is more than just competitive power. Power involves competence, achievement, and mastery. Our genetic instruction is to achieve, to master new skills, to be competent, and to be recognized for our accomplishments. The universal human genetic instruction to be competent and to accomplish is especially important for us as educators. If you come to believe that choice theory is an accurate explanation of human behavior, you accept the notion that people are structured to seek competence.

When we consider the mission of schools, it is comforting to know that what we are trying to do is consistent with how humans are structured. [In a later chapter, we will have the chance to consider if our practices support our mission and are compatible with how humans are genetically instructed to live their lives.]

Many adults, including many educators, have some difficulty believing that humans are genetically instructed to achieve. Instead, they believe that humans would likely do virtually nothing to advance themselves if it were not for external forces.

Right now, I would ask you to think about some of the truly amazing things we have in our world. Our telecommunications network is one example that comes to mind. The fax machine is a piece of technology that astounds me. The word processor on which I write these words is something else adding quality to my life. Most of these things were not created as part of a test or term project. We create and seek power and competence because the genetic instruction we have to expand our capabilities burns in our minds and hearts.

As educators, let us remember that every human, regardless of their developmental or cognitive level, wants to learn how to be more skilled, more competent. We can see it in the newborn. It expresses itself in the preschooler on a regular basis. When we respect that universal human need in our classrooms, students discover healthy, responsible ways to increase their sense of power in the world. They are less likely to be driven to get power "over" other people in destructive ways and more likely to become powerful beings who make valuable contributions to our world.

Those who advocate a back-to-basics, rigorous curriculum recognize that all human beings need to achieve in order to feel good about themselves. While love and acceptance are necessary for happiness, they are not enough. Developing new skills and abilities helps us satisfy our inborn need for power—critically important in our quest for happiness.

■ **FREEDOM** Freedom involves the ability to make choices. We are fortunate to live in a society that offers us considerable freedom, and most of us make countless choices every day. As humans, we have been genetically programmed to choose. Other creatures have been given more prescriptive genetic instructions meaning they deviate very little. In turn, their species does not change very much. Making decisions and having choices is part of what it is to be human. One of our jobs is to help others follow that genetic instruction to be free in a way that is responsible and respectful of others.

When people hear about the need for freedom for the first time, they sometimes grow uncomfortable. "Oh, no," they may think to themselves, "here comes another counselor telling us that people need to be free and can't be restricted by legitimate rules and structure." Please know that I believe some rules add quality to our lives and structure is helpful to most of us as we attempt to figure out how to best live our lives. I do not believe we necessarily need to provide people with more freedom than they currently have. What is crucial, however, is that I help those around me appreciate and become consciously aware of the many freedoms they do have. People who perceive themselves to be relatively free will not be pathologically driven to satisfy that need. People who perceive themselves as having insufficient freedom, on the other hand, will behave in ways designed to get the freedom they believe they need.

As teachers, we give our students many opportunities to satisfy the genetic instruction to be free, but we do not bring this fact to their awareness often enough. It is our job to create limits and parameters that support a quality learning environment, but we can do it in such a way that our students realize that they can meet the need for freedom easily in our classrooms.

■ **FUN** The remaining basic need, but not the least important, is fun—the genetic instruction to be playful. It is our playfulness and sense of discovery that allows us to learn as much as we do. In fact, fun is what we experience each time we learn something new. The intimate connection between fun and learning is particularly important in schools. Choice theory suggests that learning is fun. An extension of that is that the classrooms involving the most learning are the ones that are the most fun. Just as power is best understood in a general way that encompasses more than simply competition, fun does not exclusively mean outright hilarity. Fun involves the wonder, excitement, and joy we experience whenever we learn anything that is new, at least for us.

As a fifth grade student, my son had an experience that helped me appreciate the relationship between learning and fun. After dinner one night, I was doing some work on the computer and Greg was sitting in another part of the family room doing something with a paper and pencil.

"Hey!" he exclaimed, "that's cool."

I said nothing and continued my work.

Several minutes later he said, "Wow! I think it really does work. Look at this. I think I just discovered a pattern."

He then showed me some fractions that he had been multiplying. His "discovery" was cross-cancelling, a form of simplification.

"Who taught you that?" I asked.

"No one. Is it true?" he asked, not sure if his "discovery" would work all the time.

When I assured him that he had discovered something that was well established in mathematics and something I didn't learn until it was taught to me in a later grade, Greg beamed. A few days later, I asked him if he would label his new learning and "discovery" as fun.

"Absolutely," he said. "It's always fun when you learn something new."

Structured fun can help make schools exciting places where students can learn and follow their genetic instruction to be playful, have fun, and make new discoveries.

My genetic make-up instructed me to grow to a certain height, to have blue eyes, to have easily-observed physical characteristics. Choice theory suggests that I was given genetic instructions that have governed my behavior as well. Those instructions are: to love, to be powerful, to be free, and to be playful. These instructions are universal. We may not have these needs in equal amounts, just as some of us are short and some tall, some light-skinned and some dark-skinned. But all of us have some need to love, to be powerful, to be free, and to be playful. These universal genetic instructions or basic needs are what link us together as members of the same species.

### The Quality World

While our genetic instructions are universal and link us to all others, each of us is a unique individual. Our individuality is conceptualized by something called our "quality world." A very tiny part of our memory, our quality world is made up of our most treasured memories and creative musings. It includes special people, behaviors, and ideas we especially value.

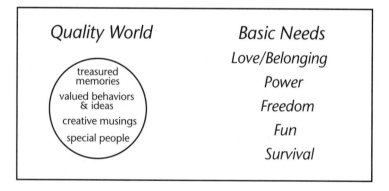

We are born with our genetic instructions and basic needs, but our quality world is empty at birth. Through need-satisfying contact with others from the time we are infants, we begin to construct our quality world. This represents how the world would be if we could have everything just as we wanted it. Everything that we place in our quality world relates to one or more of the basic needs. It is precisely because this person, activity, or value is need-satisfying that it becomes part of our quality world. Remember, too, that each of us constructs a quality world that is unique. There may be considerable overlap, but no two individuals, even identical twins share all of the pictures in their quality worlds.

Take the need for love as an example. Right now, think of a person that you love who loves you. It is important that the relationship be a reciprocal one and not pure fantasy. Most likely, you are not thinking of someone in my family, someone in my quality world. My wife and I both have our three children in our quality worlds, one area where we overlap. But each of us has people in our lives one of us values more than the other.

While the quality world is always relatively small, different people have quality worlds that are somewhat larger or smaller. What is necessary is that we each develop a quality world picture for each of the basic needs. As I said earlier, some pictures relate to multiple needs. With my wife, I am able to easily meet each of my basic needs. She is a person I love. I meet my need for personal power in our relationship, not because I have power *over* her, but because we maintain an environment where I can grow in competence, as a husband, parent, and professional. I am more free in my relationship with my wife than in any other relationship I have. And I have fun with my wife and learn from her regularly. Because I am able to follow my genetic instructions so easily in my relationship with my wife, I have a satisfying marriage.

Not everything in our quality world addresses each need area. Just as important, this does not mean that quality-world picture is of less value to us. Because of my current role with my children, who are still relatively young and living at home, I am not always as free around them as I might like. It's easy for me to follow my other genetic instructions with them (to be loving, competent, and playful), but the parental role I have chosen and created for myself sometimes mitigates against freedom. That does not mean I value my children any less. It does mean, however, that I need to look elsewhere to find places where I can follow the genetic instruction to be free without compromising my goals.

An important aspect of everything in our quality world is trust. The more we trust others, the more likely they have a prominent place in our quality world. Conversely, it is painful to have our quality world filled with people who we don't believe we can trust. This doesn't mean that people in our quality world are perfect or never let us down. It does mean, however, that when all is said and done, we want to trust those in our quality world.

What we put in our quality world is what we are willing to work for. If you think something is in your quality world and you won't work for it, think again. We work for these things because we believe that they add quality to our lives. Consider how much work some of us put into volunteer organizations, civic groups, or churches without being paid a cent. We do it and we do it gladly because we have a belief that these activities and what they represent enrich us in ways that money alone could never do. That's why many of us stay in teaching and continue to work with energy and enthusiasm—it's certainly not the pay. But people don't work *just* for pay. We work hard at things we believe will add quality to our lives. The reverse is equally true. All of us, I imagine, would like to receive healthy pay raises. Even if we were given a 15 percent raise next year, we would not necessarily work any harder. We would only do so if we believed that working harder would add quality to our lives.

■ **HOW WE BUILD OUR QUALITY WORLD** Since our quality world is empty at birth, we need to build it over time. In the normal course of events, we regularly add and delete pictures from our quality world. While the basic needs remain constant, the pictures we develop to meet those needs change over time. I often ask teachers to think of something they did when they were younger that represented fun at that time but no longer holds any appeal. The answer I hear most often is going to an amusement park. Riding the roller coaster may have been great fun in our youth, but many of us no longer hold that picture in our quality world today. Since the need for fun continues to exist, we have to constantly add new pictures to our quality world.

In the same way, we continue to need to create a sense of connection and belonging with others to satisfy our need for love. Many of us have lost track of former "best friends" over time. These people who once were prominent in our quality world have "disappeared" from our memories, and even though we might enjoy seeing them at a reunion or receiving an occasional bit of news, they no longer mean as much to us as they once did. Our quality world is always in some state of evolution, although we may achieve a state of relative stability in our adults years.

■ **CONFLICTS IN THE QUALITY WORLD** The criteria for putting something into your quality world is simply that it feels good and is need-satisfying. This brings us to a couple of significant points about the quality world. As important as it is, the quality world is not without its difficulties. Sometimes when I behave in a way that helps me follow one genetic instruction, it makes it more difficult to follow another. For example, I feel free when I am on my bicycle, alone on a country road in Cape Cod. As satisfying as that experience is, it is difficult to satisfy the need for belonging at that time. Similarly, I feel competent and a sense of personal power when I conduct a quality school training session, but that often brings me a thousand miles from home, making it harder to satisfy the belonging need with the people I love most, my family.

How are these internal conflicts best handled? The crucial factor is balance. The psychologically healthy person finds a way to satisfy all of the basic needs on a regular basis. Because you know that you will create opportunities to responsibly follow your sometimes competing quality world pictures, you can delay gratification when that is helpful as well.

> *Note: Strictly speaking, the basic needs are never "in conflict." To be "in conflict" suggests motivation and will. The basic needs are simply biological forces urging us to satisfy certain needs. What is "in conflict" are the specific quality world pictures we sometimes develop.*

A final challenge concerning the quality world relates to the fact that quality world pictures are not necessarily responsible or good for us. For something to be placed in my quality world it need only feel good and satisfy one or more needs. I can find ways to meet my needs responsibly or less responsibly. I can express my need to be powerful by striving to build a better world—to positively contribute to my community in a number of ways. I can also be powerful by dominating others and making it difficult for them to succeed. I can humiliate to get power over others.

An extreme but commonly seen example of a destructive quality world picture involves what happens to the actively-drinking alcoholic. For too many alcoholics, after a period of time their quality world shrinks and shrinks, leaving only enough room for a bottle. They only feel in control and able to satisfy their needs when drinking. Separated from alcohol, they have almost no behaviors available that help them responsibly follow their genetic instructions to love, to be powerful, to be free, and to be playful. Even if they succeed in giving up their drinking, many "dry drunks" live in horrible pain because their quality world has literally shrunk and their arsenal of behaviors has been depleted. That is why recovery is such a long and difficult process.

The quality world is where our energy resides. It is when we are with these people, doing these things, that we are most easily able to behave in a way that lets us follow our genetic instructions. Before moving on, I encourage you to pause and consider the following question: What is in your quality world?

## The Real World and The Perceived World

Somewhere out there is the real world. Ironically, in many ways the real world is unimportant when we are trying to figure out what motivates behavior. While the real world exists, what we experience is the world as we discern it, the perceived world.

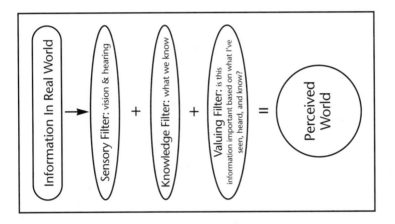

### ■ FILTERING INFORMATION FROM THE REAL WORLD

While theoretically the perceived world can match the real world, it usually differs somewhat because information must pass through at least three filters on its journey from the real world to the world we create in our heads.

**SENSORY FILTER** The first thing that distorts information coming from the real world, at least to some degree, is our sensory limitations. Regardless of how in tact my senses are, there is no such thing as perfect vision or perfect hearing. Original information is dulled and distorted to a certain degree because of the imperfections and limitations of my sensory system. Referees make calls based upon what they see. Teachers treat students based upon what they see and hear. If I don't receive the information on a sensory level, it's like it never occurred, at least in my perceived world.

**KNOWLEDGE FILTER** Information then passes through what is called our total knowledge filter. A natural human function is to try to make sense of the world. We are meaning-makers, and one way this tendency manifests itself is by trying to make sense out of incoming information based upon the knowledge we currently have. Very often we have adequate existing knowledge and the information is not distorted in any appreciable way. For example, when I am driving my car and I see that the rear lights on the car in front of me begin to glow a bright red, I know from past experience that the driver has applied the brakes. This knowledge serves me well and I choose to do the same. Even when our information is flawed or incomplete, we automatically use it the best we can.

Let me illustrate. As a third grade student, my daughter Melanie was learning about the Pilgrims. She came upon the following question on a homework assignment: "Explain why the Pilgrims had a hard time living off the land?" Melanie's knowledge base was such that she understood the phrase "living off the land" to mean "living somewhere other than land, for example a boat." Once Melanie had the phrase "living off the land" explained to her, her perception of the question changed dramatically. We can influence perception by adding new information to the total knowledge filter.

**VALUING FILTER** Finally, information passes through our valuing filter. We assign a value to every bit of information we encounter. We can assign a positive, negative, or neutral value to the information, depending upon our belief that it will be need-satisfying to us *at that moment*. We are constantly bombarded with incoming information, and much of it has very little impact upon us—at least as far as we can tell.

This information is assigned a neutral value with very little or no distortion involved.

For example, as I drive to work, I notice other cars on the road. Almost always, this information is of little consequence and neither pleases nor displeases me. Under these conditions, I assign a neutral value to the information. If, however, I become aware that the car I see is being driven erratically and poses a possible danger, I perceive it quite differently. Not only do I recognize it as a car (total knowledge filter), but I believe it represents a threat to my safety and take precautions (valuing filter). Under other conditions, the same car may be perceived positively. If I were broken down on an infrequently travelled road and eager for some assistance, the sight of another car might be valued positively because it would represent a chance to get out of a difficult situation.

The valuing filter is of critical importance because the more strongly we value something, either positively or negatively, the more likely we are to perceive it in a way different from how others perceive it. This helps explain a common and frustrating occurrence: how two people can both look out into the "real world" and come away with very different explanations about what they see.

Let me offer a final example of how it is our perceptions that matter most to us, not the real world. When I was a sophomore in college, I was asked to read *On Becoming A Person* by Carl Rogers in one of my education courses. I have always been someone who underlines when he reads, and I make innocuous little notes in the margins. At that time in my life, I was underlying in red ink. I underlined quite a bit and wrote little comments in the margins like "Yes," "Exactly," and "I agree." While you might question the depth of my thinking, at least you can appreciate that I was in agreement with what Rogers was saying. Two years later, the same book was assigned in a separate course. I was now underlining in black ink. (I'll leave it up to you to decide if this has important psychological implications.) This time, I was more impressed with other passages and sections and underlined them accordingly. My comments in the margins certainly reflected a new set of perceptions: "This is wrong," "Absolutely not," and "I disagree" provide a fair sample. Finally, I was asked to read *On Becoming A Person* one more time, this time in graduate school. I underlined different sections once again, and my comments were somewhere between the enthusiasm of sophomore year and the cynicism of senior year. The real world, the actual printed words that make up *On Becoming A Person*, did not change one bit over the years. As I added new knowledge and adjusted my values, however, my perceptions changed significantly. Like most of us, I thought that my *current* perceptions were accurate, even if they were inconsistent with what I once thought.

I take information in from the real world through my senses, understand it based upon my current knowledge, and evaluate it based on my personal values. Hopefully the perception I end up with approximates the information that exists "purely" out there in the real world. Whether it accurately represents the real world experience or not is largely irrelevant. I will live my life based upon the perceptions I develop. It is the perceived world that matters to me as I figure out how to best live my life.

■ **THE COMPARING PLACE** Every moment our brains are comparing two perceptions:

- The quality world picture we have of how we would like the world to be at that moment.

- Our perception of what is real at that moment.

As we compare these two perceptions, we automatically evaluate how closely the two pictures match. If the two are reasonably similar, our internal scales remain essentially balanced and we get an internal signal that tells us our life is in pretty good order, at least for the moment. If, on the other hand, the two perceptions are sufficiently different from one anoth-

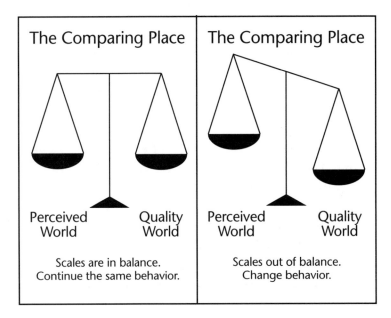

| The Comparing Place | The Comparing Place |
| --- | --- |
| Perceived World — Quality World | Perceived World — Quality World |
| Scales are in balance. Continue the same behavior. | Scales out of balance. Change behavior. |

er, our internal scales are tipped and we get a power-ful internal signal that tells us something is wrong.

Imagine you are a math teacher, introducing a new concept to your students. You are working at the chalkboard, illustrating a point you believe is impor-tant. Whether you ever heard of choice theory before this is unimportant. All teachers have a quality world picture of what a class should look like at times like this. The specifics might vary, but teachers typically want the students to be attentive, to be engaged by the material, and to demonstrate through their behaviors that they are beginning to understand the concept you are presenting. As you observe the class, you find that your perception of what is going on closely matches your quality world picture. Your scales are balanced. You get a strong "YES!" signal and you continue to present the material in much the same way. If, howev-er, your perception of the class is substantially differ-ent from the quality world picture you have, your scales will be tipped. You will get a strong "NO!" sig-nal, and you will likely change your approach.

The comparing place is where everything happens in choice theory. It is where internal self-evaluation takes place and we evaluate if what we are doing is working well enough for us to be satisfied. Change only occurs when the scales are tipped sufficiently. I will only change my behavior when I come to the conclusion that the world I perceive is so different from the world I want that it is worthwhile to put forth the effort required to behave differently. One of two things must occur to get my scales to tip:

- I must have a change in perception, perhaps because new information has been introduced that impacts my perception; or,

- I must change my quality world picture so that what I perceive no longer adequately matches my newly-developed want.

The internal signal we get, indicating that our scales are in balance or out of balance, initiates our behaviors. Choice theory teaches us that all we can do as living organisms is behave. We literally cannot *not behave*. As I mentioned earlier, if the signal suggests that we are getting pretty much what we want, we are driven to behave in a similar fashion.

If my classes are going well, I will continue to teach in much the same way. If I perceive that my marriage is going well, I will continue to conduct myself in the same ways in that relationship. If I successfully shoot five free throws in a row, I will continue to shoot the same way.

When the scales are tipped, I am still driven to behave, but because of the negative feedback I am getting, I am likely to choose to behave differently. The discomfort that might be involved in generating sufficient energy to behave differently seems preferable to the pain of continuing to behave in the same way with the same unsatisfying results. Let's go back to the example of the math teacher introducing a new concept. If things were not going very much like you wanted, your scales would be tipped and you would search for alternative behaviors.

It is helpful to remember two basic reality therapy principles:

- All behavior is purposeful.
- Everybody is doing the best they can.

This is not to say that all behavior is effective or responsible, but it is always purposeful. Regardless of what you choose to do when you make the evaluation that the class is not going well, your choice is always made with the idea that the new behavior will help get your scales back in balance. How effective and responsible your behavior is will be determined by what behaviors you have available to you (everybody is doing the best they can). As lifelong learners, we are continually trying to find better, more responsible, more effective ways to behave when we find ourselves in that uncomfortable place where scales are tipped.

■ **TOTAL BEHAVIOR** The subject of behavior has been studied in great detail by Dr. Glasser. One of his major contributions in understanding human motivation relates to the description of what he calls "total behavior." Glasser highlighted the fact that all behavior is made up of four components. Most people identify behaviors by their most obvious or dominant component, but all four components are present in every behavior. This is why choice theorists refer to all behavior as total behavior. The four components of total behavior are: acting, thinking, feeling, and physiology. Choice theory teaches us that when you change any one component of total behavior, the other components change as well.

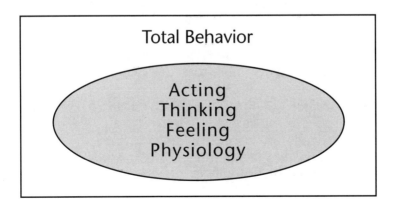

Total Behavior

Acting
Thinking
Feeling
Physiology

To illustrate the concept of total behavior more fully, let's go back to the story of Melanie and her piano lesson offered at the beginning of Part I. The evening after I had spoken to her about the piano lesson, I asked Melanie if she were still "choosing to be nervous." "Oh, no," she said. "That's all over now." After telling Melanie how happy I was that she had experienced such relief, I told her it was really important for me to know how she was able to be successful. Melanie's comments were a wonderful illustration of the concept of total behavior. In her own words, Melanie was "choosing to be nervous." Nervousness represents the *feeling* component of her total behavior. Even though it is difficult to feel better just because we want to, whenever we are in a state of discomfort we behave in ways designed to help us feel better. When I asked Melanie how she was able to give up "choosing to be nervous," she began by focusing upon the *acting* component of total behavior: "Well, talking last night really helped." She then brought up the *thinking* component of total behavior: "Also, I spent some time thinking about what we said, and when I went to bed I just thought about how I didn't need to be nervous."

I was satisfied that Melanie had given me what I hoped to hear by referring to the two components of behavior over which we have most arbitrary control: acting and thinking. Still, as I continue to practice reality therapy, I have learned to ask, "Anything else?" Melanie then brought in the *physiological* aspect of total behavior when she said, "Well, I don't know really. But it just seemed that after I had a good sleep, I woke up and didn't feel nervous anymore." A refreshing sleep altered Melanie's physiology, impacting the other components of her total behavior.

■ **CHANGING OUR ACTING AND THINKING** The purpose of our behavior is to help us *feel* better. Paradoxically, we have little direct impact on our feelings. It's hard to feel better just because we want to or to feel less bored simply because we want to.

However, we almost always have some control over our *acting and thinking,* two other components of total behavior. When we significantly change our acting or thinking, we are changing our total behavior, and our feelings and physiology change as well. In Melanie's case, the conversation we had (acting) and the reflection she did (thinking), coupled with a good night's sleep (physiology) eliminated her nervousness (feelings). Those of us who practice reality therapy generally focus our efforts on the acting and thinking because they are the components of total behavior that we can consciously change with the greatest ease. This does not mean it is always easy to change our acting and thinking; but it is almost always *easier* than trying to change our feelings and physiology directly.

The concept of total behavior is one of the most important and powerful concepts in choice theory. It allows us to take full responsibility for our lives. Once Melanie realized that her "nervousness" was really a choice she was making, she was able to make a more satisfying choice.

When you accept the concept of total behavior and internalize it, you will travel on a challenging pathway. You become unable to easily play the role of passive victim. A headache will no longer be something you just "get." It will be perceived as the physiological component of a total behavior that you can control to a large extent. What actions are you taking, how are you living your life and managing stress that you experience this headache? While it is demanding and sometimes uncomfortable to confront ourselves in such a direct way, it is also the most liberating, exhilarating path I have encountered. Once I honestly self-evaluate, I can almost always figure out other ways to act and think that will lead to a physiological state different from the headache I experience.

The next time you experience emotional or physiological discomfort, experiment with the concept of total behavior and see if you can discover actions and thoughts that will lead to a relief of your pain. It is not enough to talk about responsibility; we need to act in a responsible way.

## THE VALUE OF THE CHOICE THEORY MODEL

The behavior we choose to perform in the real world is always purposeful. It is designed to restore balance, to act in the world so what I perceive closely approximates what I want. This process of perceiving, comparing, and acting is never-ending as we continually attempt to satisfy our basic needs and follow the genetic instructions to love, to be powerful, to be free, and to be playful.

Choice theory is valuable because it provides us a model for understanding human behavior. It helps us appreciate that human beings are active, not reactive. It teaches us that we are internally motivated, not controlled by outside events or stimuli. Choice theory refutes the "common sense" model of understanding human behavior: stimulus-response theory. With a firm understanding of choice theory, we can begin to build schools that are consistent with the notions of internal motivation, quality world pictures, and personal responsibility.

# CHAPTER 3

# *Reality Therapy*

While a choice theory model provides a framework for understanding human behavior, reality therapy is a process bringing choice theory principles to life. Originally developed as a counseling approach, many use reality therapy in numerous settings, including education. I like to identify reality therapy as a communication process applicable in any human interaction.

I am frequently asked if I use reality therapy *on* my own family or *on* people at work. My answer is always the same: I consciously strive to use a reality therapy approach to communication *with* everyone. Integration of choice theory ideas means that I take responsibility for my own life and behaviors. As I use reality therapy, I look into an imaginary mirror and determine if I am behaving in a way that is consistent with my quality world picture of who I want to be. In any exchange, I have a number of choices available to me. Sometimes the choices are obvious and plentiful. At other times, the choices are less obvious, and it may "feel" as if I have no choice at all. My understanding of choice theory has helped me appreciate that even in those moments *some* choice is available. Given the limitations and parameters of any situation, natural or self-chosen, I then move forward and choose those behaviors that I believe will help me move toward the type of person I wish to become. (Of course, what I have described is an idealized version. In the real world, there are many times when I behave in less intentional ways and choose behaviors not reflective of who I wish to become. Still, I accept and value the notion that my behaviors are choices and the resulting consequences are always my responsibility.)

Reality therapy is made up of two components:

1. The environment that surrounds any relationship.

2. The actual procedures used in an interaction with another.

Let's examine each of these components in some detail.

## THE ENVIRONMENT

When talking about the nature of a relationship in reality therapy, the first major issue discussed is referred to as "involvement." Involvement entails creating a relationship that demonstrates genuine caring for the other. It clearly communicates to the other that I am here to help you achieve more quality in your life. Involvement includes being friendly, but it is much more than that. We all know people with whom we are friendly, but with whom we have little genuine involvement. When we are truly involved with another, we become part of each other's quality worlds. We value each other and care about each other.

When you are in a relationship with another and things are not working as well as you would like, the involvement is not strong enough. To improve the relationship, work on building the involvement. Utilizing choice theory and reality therapy principles, take responsibility for *your* behavior and strengthen the involvement. Without those skills, you would most likely put your effort into changing the other person. Paradoxically that would only weaken the involvement, damage the relationship, and you would be less satisfied in the long run.

When involvement is discussed in reality therapy, it is often further clarified by the term "role involvement." Role involvement emphasizes the fact that the nature of my involvement with you will be somewhat determined by the roles we have relative to each other.

For example, when I conduct a workshop, as a participant you accept a particular role. How we relate to each other during our time together will be defined to a large extent by those roles. There are certain behaviors you can rightfully expect of me and other behaviors that you would not expect me to exhibit. Over time we may choose to change our relationship and develop a friendship outside of the workshop setting. As our roles change, so does the quality of our involvement. This is not to suggest that different kinds of involvement are "better" than others. Rather, it simply clarifies that how we appropriately relate to each other is in part determined by the nature of our roles relative to each other.

Role involvement is a concept particularly important in education. In order to get to a point where we can effectively teach more students than we currently do, we need to develop strong involvement with them. At the same time, as teachers, we intentionally adopt a set of behaviors appropriate to and consistent with our role. A reality therapy approach to education does not mean that you need to become best friends with your students. In fact, I would suggest that teachers and students not be "best friends." In my vision of a quality school, teachers are mentors or coaches. They have recognized expertise that they are eager to share. The nature of the relationship is not, however, one of equals. The teacher and student each value the other, respect the other, and put each other in their quality worlds. But the nature of their role involvement is such that they will not likely be best friends. At some point, both parties may decide that the relationship would be more satisfying if they shifted it to one of friendship, but when they do that, they will no longer be primarily student and teacher or mentor. There is a difference between being friendly and being friends. Involvement suggests that you be friendly with the other; it does not imply that you be friends with everyone.

How would a relationship between a teacher and student look if it were characterized by strong role involvement? I would ask you to take some time right now and think about your vision of what that relationship would be like. If it would be helpful, make yourself some written notes. This is not a trivial exercise. Instead, it is an opportunity for you to specifically develop *your* quality world picture of an idealized, appropriate teacher-student relationship. The specifics of that quality world picture will vary from teacher to teacher because it is an expression of our individuality. The pictures will vary, too, because we work with students of different ages with different developmental tasks. Behavior that would be appropriate in one setting may be counterproductive in another. What is important is that we clearly identify our unique vision of the relationship we believe is most appropriate to have with our students.

Later I will suggest a model that will get you together with colleagues and compare ideas, making sure that you maintain your individuality without setting up visions that have you working at cross-purposes with others in your building.

The concept of role involvement can and should be considered as you examine all of your professional relationships. Using the same process, think about and develop your vision of an idealized, appropriate relationship with other teachers, department heads, building level administrators, central office personnel, paraprofessionals, and parents. While you cannot control how anyone else behaves, this process will provide you a vision of how you want to behave in these relationships. This is an important step in taking personal responsibility for our own lives.

## Present-Tense Orientation

Using the principles of reality therapy, we focus our attention on the present when dealing with others. Some people mistakenly believe that those of us who practice reality therapy ignore the past and its importance.

As I heard Dr. Glasser say one time:

> We are all products of our past. In reality therapy we simply believe that we do not need to be *prisoners* of our past.

Those of us who regularly apply the principles of reality therapy do our best to make sure that we really put into practice the idea that "today is a new day." Students begin each day with a clean slate and we create an environment designed to help them become more successful and responsible.

Being focused on the present does not mean that we ignore the past. There are at least two instances when reference to the past is especially helpful:

- The past always needs to be dealt with when it continues to actively impact the present. In such cases, failure to address those issues that originate in the past will only worsen the situation.

- The past is also fertile ground to consider when it represents an area where someone has been successful.

There is no reason to re-invent the wheel each time a problem is encountered. Imagine, for example, that you are working with a student who is in danger of failing a course required for graduation. It is helpful to ask, "Have you ever been in a situation like this before where you successfully figured out what to do?" Even if the *exact* same strategy may not be effective this time around, past successes can be used as building blocks in current situations.

Avoiding the past in this context essentially means that we reject the idea of bringing up past failures to others. Those reminders only serve to weaken self-esteem, confirm a negative identity, and perpetuate the failure already experienced.

Again I would ask you to take few minutes right now for reflection. Remember a time when your past failures were brought to your attention, perhaps with sarcasm, at least with disapproval. In most cases, isn't it true that you already knew about your shortcomings and learned nothing helpful when told about things that you could not go back and remedy?

- How did you feel at that moment?
- Were those feelings helpful to you in your growth?

In most cases, you will probably agree that the reference to past failure is certainly not helpful and quite likely counterproductive. Even if you can think of instances where you believed it was helpful, I would challenge you by asking if it is possible to imagine another, less potentially damaging way to make progress. Remember, too, that many of our students bring fragile, tenuous self-concepts to the classroom. The less successful they have been, the less resilient they are and the more likely they will be at risk when repeatedly confronted by their past failures. It would be far less risky and more productive to dedicate our energy to the present and help students develop more successful and responsible behaviors *starting now.*

### Don't Be Overwhelmed By the Problem

Most of us become teachers because we genuinely care about children. As a group, educators are caring and sensitive and want their students to have wonderful lives. An unfortunate reality is that some of our students come from very difficult situations. Many have faced serious deprivation at an early age. Some have had to deal with a cruel and inexplicable death of a family member. Some live in poverty. Others are surrounded by crime, drugs, and other horrors no child should have to face. Still others are raised in homes where there is little love and affection expressed appropriately. When we become involved with such children, it is easy to become overwhelmed by their truly painful stories. Our "nice" side feels the pain suffered by these unfortunate children.

Using reality therapy, we work hard not to become overwhelmed by these horrible stories. It's not that we want to deny the emotional horror and behave in a desensitized, robotic way; when we become overwhelmed, however, we lose our capacity to effectively help these children forge a better life for themselves. I have heard teachers say things like, "It's no wonder she doesn't do any homework. When you look at what she has to endure every day when she goes home, it's amazing that she even gets herself here at all." The problem with comments like that is that they unconsciously create an atmosphere of pity likely to perpetuate the problem. What children need is our strength and help in finding ways to make things better. Pity by itself will feel good for a brief period, but will not help students find their way to a better place.

■ **A WORD OF CAUTION** When dealing with especially difficult situations, never tell another person you *understand* what they are going through or feeling. Even if you have experienced something ostensibly similar, it is a disrespectful assumption to imagine that your experience mirrors theirs. Of course if you have never had a similar experience, you have even less reason to say, "I understand what you're going through. I know how you feel." You don't. How do you handle such situations then? I find myself using a three-part process:

1. I acknowledge that I don't know what the other is experiencing.

2. I affirm what they are telling me, respecting their current status.

3. Once I believe I have developed enough involvement to proceed, I ask them if they would like to

make things better and I offer my support and help.

Even people from horrible situations have found ways to build meaningful, successful lives. "Would you like to be one of those people?" I ask. This allows a person in pain to begin to develop a quality world picture that will ultimately serve as the motivation to build a more satisfying life.

Every person deserves that chance. By not becoming overwhelmed when I work with difficult cases, I foster an environment where dreams can begin to take root.

## Accept No Excuses For Irresponsible Behavior

When interacting with another and utilizing a reality therapy approach, never accept excuses for irresponsible behaviors. This does not mean you would refuse to listen to a reasonable explanation. There are times when all of us have legitimate reasons why we cannot do what we fully expected to do. Unforeseen circumstances do arise and the practitioner of reality therapy is accepting of those inconveniences. In contrast, an excuse is when someone begins to create a rationale designed to absolve them of responsibility.

*Remember: a central goal in reality therapy is to help people develop responsible behaviors.*

Quite unintentionally, when we accept excuses for irresponsible behavior, we are telling the other person that it is OK to behave in less responsible ways. When we accept excuses we may even communicate to the other that we never really expected them to follow through, further eroding an already fragile self-esteem.

## Avoid Punishment And Criticism

Even though you never want to accept excuses, it is equally important to never criticize or punish when dealing with others. Criticism is an especially damaging behavior and one used with regularity. In fact, we are so taken by the alleged value of criticism that we sanitize this counterproductive behavior by calling it "constructive criticism."

Think about a time when you were criticized. The odds are you were not feeling a tremendous amount of love and belonging, at least at the moment of the criticism. What about power? It's hard to feel a sense of competence and achievement when you are being criticized. Freedom? Especially if you were being criticized by a person with some authority, you most likely did not believe you could have easily walked out. Even if that choice were available, the consequences might have been seen as particularly costly, so you were left believing you had very little freedom. Finally, there is the need for fun. It is hard to follow the genetic instruction to be playful while you are being criticized. When you are being criticized it is virtually impossible to satisfy your needs. Not surprisingly, we frequently take criticizers out of our quality worlds if they were there in the beginning. Of course, when we have little or no involvement with the other, the criticism all but assures that that person will never be part of our quality world.

■ **HOW DANGEROUS IS CRITICISM?** Can criticism ever be tolerated? As horrible as criticism is, strong relationships can tolerate a degree of criticism. Keep this in mind, though: criticism *never* helps the relationship improve in quality.

Here's an example of what I mean. In my opinion, the relationship which has the greatest chance of approaching the ideal is an adult love relationship. In my case, that means my relationship with my wife. We developed our relationship as adults and brought well-developed identities to each other. Each of us had already established a strong sense of values and notions about what it meant to live a quality life. In our 21 years of marriage, I have *never once been helped by my wife's criticism! And my criticism has never helped her!* It is true that sometimes our relationship has grown stronger after some particularly critical words.

*But is was never the criticism that brought us to that place of greater quality. It was all the hard work and cleaning up we did after the critical comments were made.* I firmly believe we could have arrived at that better place more quickly and with less pain if we were willing to give up the criticism.

A strong, solid marriage, can withstand a certain amount of criticism. But remember, that's a relationship that has developed considerable strength over a period of time. What about relationships with others, specifically at school? No matter how popular you are with students or how much you care for them, you do not have the same position of prominence in their quality world as a husband and wife do. If criticism is strong enough to destroy a marriage (and it has in many cases), imagine how easily criticism can destroy a relationship between you and a student or you and a colleague.

■ **DOES CRITICISM EVER WORK?** As destructive as criticism is, it would be untrue to say it can *never* be used effectively. A prime example is provided in the movie *Stand and Deliver* about Jaime Escalante and his work with inner city Hispanic students learning calculus. Throughout the movie, the character playing Escalante criticizes and berates the students, engaging in name-calling and other seemingly degrading behaviors. Through it all, the students continue to work hard and succeed in AP Calculus. Given the ideas of reality therapy presented here, how was Escalante able to help his students do high quality work when he criticized them in a way that would get most public educators in serious trouble? The key is that Escalante had established sufficient role involvement with his students so that his comments, heard by many of us as criticism, were perceived by the students as an expression of genuine caring. They believed that Escalante had their best interests in mind and really wanted to help them add quality to their lives. With that belief system, they filtered his comments in such a way as to hear love and caring disguised as sarcasm. By demonstrating genuine

love and concern for his students, Escalante had established himself in their quality worlds.

*A word of caution: most of us, as skilled as we might be,
cannot do what Jaime Escalante did so successfully. In the
majority of cases, the sarcasm and criticism are heard as
just that and make it unlikely that higher quality work will
ever be produced.*

Another area where criticism is used on a fairly regular basis is in athletics. Many coaches intentionally use
a lot of criticism as a "motivational tool." Again, it
often seems to work. Why? In most cases, the student
athletes have winning in their quality world. Because
the idea of winning means so much to these students,
they can tolerate the coach's criticism. While many
coaches may not agree, I believe that they could abandon the criticism and be at least as effective as they currently are precisely because the athletes want to win
already.

■ **DISCIPLINE VERSUS PUNISHMENT** Punishment, too,
is removed from the environment when you are using
a reality therapy approach. People sometimes use the
terms "punishment" and "discipline" as synonyms
when, in fact, they represent quite different concepts.

Discipline is an effective and necessary process helping people figure out how they should behave toward
each other in certain situations. When a violation of a
code of conduct occurs, we discipline to help teach the
student a better way. The goal is consistent with our
central mission as educators: we are taking advantage
of a "teachable moment" and helping the student learn
a more responsible and equally effective behavior.

Punishment, on the other hand, is used to hurt
someone else. It compromises the student's self-esteem
and does not teach a better way.

Here's one easy way to distinguish between the two
when you find yourself confused. If you find yourself
saying that the action you are taking with a student is
important "for the good of the other kids," you are
almost always in a punishment situation. Discipline
helps the student who has violated a rule. Punishment

hurts the individual student and is often justified because it will serve "the student body."

## TAKING THE TIME TO MAKE REAL CHANGE

When we talk about creating a positive environment and developing a healthy, productive relationship, it must be understood that it takes a lot of time. Early on in our relationship, we may need to spend most of our time attending to relationship or environmental concerns. At this point in the relationship, it may seem that using a reality therapy approach "takes too much time." This is a frequent concern among classroom teachers who have so much to do during the course of the day. Again, building the appropriate relationship is a wise investment. The time you spend doing this will pay big dividends over time, allowing you to teach more, and have students do higher quality work.

In the beginning of a relationship it is often necessary to spend nearly all of your time building the environment in order to become established in the other's quality world. At that point, you have little time left for the "real" work of change and the reality therapy process understandably appears slow and laborious. Over time, however, the situation can reverse so that you need spend only a fraction of your time and energy maintaining a healthy relationship, leaving plenty of time to do the more visible change work. Suddenly, reality therapy seems magically transformed into a wonderfully time-effective approach. In fact, it has little to do with magic and much to do with appreciating and honoring the importance of both building and maintaining a healthy relationship.

Of course, there will be times in any relationship when you will have to spend a significant amount of time and energy on environmental concerns. Still, it is important to know that if you build a healthy and genuine relationship, a process that seems time-consuming at first, things will flow smoothly and easily.

If you are concerned about time, I might also ask you to think about how effective and powerful it would be if an entire district adopted a reality therapy approach to interacting with students, parents, and colleagues. If you are working in isolation or relative isolation, you will no doubt need to spend an awful lot of precious time on environmental issues and building relationships. On the other hand, if you work in a system where a whole building or a whole district embraces these ideas, the environment perpetuates itself. Students will put you into their quality world easily, almost automatically, because the culture and climate of the school will support that choice.

## *The Procedures That Lead To Change*

The procedures that lead to change involve some of the specific questions and strategies related to the reality therapy process. They will be described here in one "typical" sequence, but it important to say that the order in which you cover these points is really quite flexible. If the process is relatively new to you, you may find it easier to follow this "typical" sequence for a while, until you become more comfortable. Over time, depending upon the nature of a given situation, you will find that you skip around and develop your own appropriate sequence for that particular situation.

It is also important for me to mention the importance of personal style. You have your own set of successful strategies and a style that reflects your values and personality. My hope for you would be that you can take the general procedures that lead to change and bring them to life by infusing into them your own style and genuineness. Just as we all share the same universal basic needs but develop our unique quality world, all of us using reality therapy make use of the procedures that lead to change but in a way that affirms our individual styles and personalities.

■ **ASK WHAT DO YOU WANT?** In order to help someone change, it is crucial to have them identify their wants. During this part of the process, you are trying to have the other person get a clear sense of what is in his or her quality world. Remember, it is our quality world pictures that drive us so we need to know just what we want in order to take our lives in the direction that is most appropriate for us at that time.

There are lots of ways to help people figure out what they want. The most direct might be to simply ask them, "What do you want?" While this is not a bad place to begin, don't be surprised if you encounter any one of a number of problems.

■ **DEAL WITH I DON'T KNOW** Teachers frequently run into the problem of students saying that they just don't know what they want. If that happens to you, let me suggest two possibilities.

One is that you just haven't established enough genuine involvement for students to give you a glimpse of their quality world. If you are an action-oriented person who likes to "get things done," you may be moving at a speed greater than the students can tolerate comfortably. Their way of dealing with discomfort when asked what they want is often just to say "I don't know." Remember that when you ask someone what they want, you are asking them to reveal a part of their quality world. That can be a risky proposition and leaves us vulnerable. I may not want to tell you what I really want because I'm afraid that you will either tell me that I can't have it or suggest that what I want is foolish. You might laugh at me or criticize my unsuccessful attempts to get it. In such cases, it becomes much easier to say "I don't know" and short-circuit the process. The only thing that will overcome such a roadblock is strong, genuine involvement. If I believe that you are here to help me, that you won't laugh at me, that you won't criticize me, and that you will help me add more quality to my life, then I might be willing to answer the seemingly innocuous, but really, very scary question: "What do you want?"

My experience tells me that when I hear "I don't know," it almost always means I have failed to develop sufficient involvement. Occasionally, however, I have run across students (and adults) who really did believe that they didn't know what they wanted. In those rare cases, I have found it helpful to flip the question to a negative and ask it like this: "Well, if you don't know what you do want, can you at least tell me what it is that you *don't* want?" Frequently, this switch is answered more easily and provides us with a starting point. If a student answers, "Well, I don't want to go to summer school," that gives me the chance to ask, "Does that mean that you'd like to pass your classes?" In this way, we can get to a want, albeit indirectly.

■ **DEAL WITH THE SUPERFICIAL ANSWER** We all desire many things. When you ask a person "What do you want?" don't expect that what they tell you necessarily represents the most important or significant want. It's not uncommon for people to test the waters a little bit by giving an answer that is true, but relatively superficial. Different practitioners have their own way of dealing with this issue. While some of my colleagues prefer to dig around for more significant "wants," I tend to be satisfied with lower level wants early in a relationship. I accept that the students are consciously or non-consciously testing our relationship, trying to figure out if I am a person who can help them add more quality to their lives. With that in mind, I set about working on that relatively superficial want, basing my action on the following belief: if I can be helpful to students in their quest to add even just a little quality to their lives, and if I can help them develop even one behavior that allows them to get what they want responsibly, they will begin to trust me more, take me into their quality world, and allow me to learn about some of their more significant wants as our relationship deepens.

■ **PUT THE QUESTION IN CONTEXT**  "What do you want?" can be a dangerous question if asked without a context. When I think of wants, I think of layers and possibilities defined by the context. To illustrate this point in workshops, I ask participants to do the following:

> Imagine I could magically transport you to wherever you would like to be and have you be accompanied by whomever you wished. Where would you be, who would you be with, and what would you be doing? Develop as specific a picture as you can.
>
> Now, return to the present and accept the fact that you are in this workshop, freely chosen, to learn about choice theory, reality therapy, and quality schools. Given those parameters, imagine how you would like this workshop to be. Develop a quality world picture for our time together.

The difference between the two "wants" is generally significant. It's not that one is any more honest than the other. It's just that our brains will work differently when we ask it to consider things with parameters or without.

When working with students, I find it important to contextualize the "What do you want?" question as it relates to school and my role with the student. A classroom teacher may ask, "What would you like to learn in this course, knowing that this is a math course and my job is to teach you geometry?" More specific and contextualized questions like this are generally more fruitful than the generic "What do you want?"

■ **DEAL WITH A LAUNDRY LIST OF WANTS**  It may not happen as frequently, but another situation that you may encounter when asking "What do you want?" is hearing a laundry list of wants. When this occurs, one of your first tasks is to help the other prioritize or at least figure out where to begin. Keeping in mind the principles of choice theory, this process provides you with an opportunity to build a need-satisfying environment that, in turn, helps you become established in the other's quality world. For the sake of illustration, assume you are working with a student who has a long list of wants. If I were working with the student, I would say something like this:

> It certainly sounds like you have a clear idea of some of the things you'd like. In order for me to help you, we'll have to figure out where to begin. I'm afraid if we try to do too many things at once, we'll have less success than if we focus our energy on one area at a time. So let's clarify our work.
>
> Is there something here that really *needs* to be taken care of first before we move on to something else? It might not even be the most important thing, but it's the most pressing. If not, then where would you like to have us begin our work together? What makes most sense to you? It can be the most important issue or you might rather begin with something else. All I need from you is to know that you are really committed and that you'll give this your best effort.

Notice that as you talk with a student in this way, you create a need-satisfying environment in a way that is genuine and relevant. By asking the student where she would like to begin work, you provide freedom. By respecting the student's decision and letting her choose where to begin work, you also create an environment where she can achieve power in a responsible way. In a concrete way, you are affirming that she is competent to determine where the work will begin. Finally, as you genuinely communicate caring for the student and let her know you want to work with her so that the student can add quality to her life, you foster an environment that is conducive to meeting the need for belonging.

■ **EXPLORE THE 'WANT'** When people tell you what they want, it is often helpful to explore the want with them to determine to what need or needs it relates. For example, a student may tell you that she wants to be a more successful student. I can't think of too many teachers who would not support a student's desire to achieve more academic success. It would be helpful to ask the student the following questions:

- How would your life be different if you were a better student?
- What would you have that you don't have now?

The answers she gives you will be important because they will provide you with insight as to what needs are currently less well met and what she hopes to satisfy through better academic achievement. You may hear about pleasing her parents (love and belonging), proving she can do more rigorous work (power), being given more time to be with her friends if she brings home better grades (freedom), or the joy of learning something new (fun). As you continue to work with this student, knowing what need or needs are behind her wants will help you be more effective.

There's another reason for having students identify how their life would be better if they had what they say they want. The process of talking about something we value increases our desire for it, which, in turn, increases our motivation to get it. The student who begins to talk about the increased freedom she will experience when she improves her grades is more likely to sustain her efforts than one who has not made the connection between the want and the underlying need.

Still, another reason for having someone identify how their life would be better if they had what they wanted is that it sometimes clarifies for the person why something is valued. Not infrequently, people are surprised to learn just why they value certain things. In workshops with teachers, I often ask participants to consider what need or needs teaching satisfies. Frequently, as they give this issue serious thought, participants discover that they value teaching for reasons they had never considered. Some who truly believed that they valued the profession because of the vacation time (freedom), discover that they are value working in a building where people really care about one another (love and belonging). Still others are given the chance to discover that they view themselves as competent professionals who have positively touched the lives of many children (power).

Why not take a moment to consider how your professional life provides a pathway for *you* to satisfy your needs. If you were to lose your job, what would you lose in terms of need-satisfaction? (By the way, if you share your thoughts with a group, don't be surprised if a number of equally dedicated and skilled professionals meet different needs through teaching. There's nothing "wrong" with a teacher who says that the freedom provided in our job is the thing she values most as long as she provides a classroom experience that helps children grow and learn positively. The only discovery that might be painful is to learn that teaching really offers you very little in terms of need-satisfaction. If that's the case, I can't imagine that you enjoy your job or do it in a way that reflects quality. You might actually do yourself a favor if you began to explore other careers to figure out where you could get more need-satisfaction.)

■ **WHAT ARE YOU DOING TO GET IT?** Once a want has been identified, determine what steps have been taken to achieve it. The basic reality therapy question at this point is, "What are you doing to get it?" but there are a number of variations. In all cases, however, the goal is the same: to help the other explore what steps they have taken. An important point here is to make sure that you don't turn the reality therapy process into an interrogation. Because you're seeking information, it's easy to slip into a dialogue that sounds more like an interrogation than a conversation. If you find that happening, make sure to switch gears or you will find the process becomes bogged down and ineffective. When things feel like an interrogation, they quickly become very *unsatisfying*, weakening the counseling relationship.

Often things can be improved by simply turning questions into statements. For example, "What kind of things have you tried?" can be reframed as, "Tell me some of the things you've done." "What else?" can become "That's interesting. Tell me more." Of course, there are times when asking some questions is a way of demonstrating genuine interest and involvement. As you practice the process more intentionally, listen to yourself. Finally, I learned the following strategy from some colleagues. I often tell students that part of my job is to ask questions, establishing my role with them. I then tell them that their job is to decide which questions they will answer. This structure clarifies our roles, gives the student responsible ways to get power and freedom in our interaction, and prepares them for the questioning that follows.

Notice your tone of voice. Is it inviting, involving, and conveying the notion that you are there to help the others responsibly get more of what they want? If not, try to figure out how you can become more like the person you would like to be in this interaction. It is equally important to become increasingly sensitive to non-verbal communication. Notice your body language. Pretend for a moment that you were the other person. What type of presentation do you make? Do you seem interested, involved, caring, bored, judgmental? What qualities would *you* find helpful in someone else if you were looking for help? Do you already have some of those characteristics? Can you add a few more to your repertoire so you can be more effective?

---

### Self-Evaluation

If there is one component in the process of reality therapy that distinguishes it from every other counseling approach—the concept of self-evaluation. After identifying both the want (quality world picture) and present behaviors, you ask the other person to evaluate the effectiveness of their behaviors. The self-evaluation question asks: "Does your current behavior have a reasonable chance of helping you get what you want responsibly, both now and in the long run?"

For obvious reasons, the questions is almost never asked in that exact way. If you were ever to present that much verbal information to most children, they would have forgotten most of the beginning of the question by the time you reached the end of the question. Still, each part of the self-evaluation question as presented is important. As I look at it, there are three separate issues that the question addresses:

■ **SIMPLE EVALUATION** The first is self-evaluation in the simplest sense. This part of the question simply asks, "Is it working?" "How has it been going?" or "On a scale of 1 to 10, how successful would you rate yourself?"

■ **RESPONSIBILITY** The second component to the more global self-evaluation question introduces the concept of responsibility. Because reality therapy is a process used to help people learn to behave in responsible ways, self-evaluation needs to be discussed in that context. A criminal may evaluate his behavior as very successful as he continues to commit robberies and elude the police, but his behavior is not responsible because it interferes with other people's attempts to satisfy their needs. Similarly, the playground bully might self-evaluate and declare that his coercive behaviors, designed to extort money from younger, smaller students is working, but he would have a harder time characterizing it as responsible behavior.

■ **RAMIFICATIONS** Finally, the issue of self-evaluation must consider both the immediate and longer-term ramifications of behavioral choices. By their very nature, children are often unable to appreciate the long-term consequences of their actions. Many of them can't see much beyond the present. For these children, it is critically important to explore the long-term consequences of their behaviors. Let's take the case of a student who plays the role of class clown in the seventh grade. To ask the simple evaluation question, "Is it working?" is not enough. Stuck in the present, the student may answer, "Of course it's working." If you have taught him something about the basic psychological needs, he may even be able to articulate how his current behavior helps him to satisfy his needs:

> When I fool around in class, I don't mean anything by it. It's just for kicks (fun). Besides, other kids tell me they think I'm funny and want to hang around with me (belonging). Anyway, it gets boring always doing what the teacher wants you to do (freedom) and half the time I don't even know what he's talking about (power).

Looked at from a short-term, present-tense orientation, it's easy to understand *why* the student has taken on the role of class clown. It satisfies multiple needs and looked at from this perspective, the student self-evaluates and determines that the behaviors involved in being a class clown are worthwhile. That's where you need to intervene as a responsible adult with the capacity to appreciate the possible long-term negative consequences. By exploring the future, you help the student discover that the class clown role may have only short-term appeal.

Don't think that by simply bringing up the future, children (or adults) will automatically change their behaviors. Remember, choice theory teaches us that *all* behavior is purposeful and represents the individual's best attempt at that moment to meet his or her needs. If class clown behaviors are being chosen, they are being chosen for a reason, and the simple exploration of the long-term consequences will generally not be enough to change the patterns right away. If that were the case, life would be much easier. Insight, or making the unconscious conscious, is not all that is needed. I have never worked with a student in such a situation who realized the possible long-term negative consequences of his behavior for the first time and said to me, "I never thought of that before. I'll never do that again." But I have had them experience some discomfort as they considered the future for the first time. And that discomfort is the beginning of the tipping of the scales necessary to initiate genuine behavioral change.

Self-evaluation is the cornerstone of reality therapy and what makes it both unique and powerful. All counseling approaches have their own jargon and way of doing things. In reality therapy, we talk about the *quality world* and the importance of determining what the other person wants. While the term *quality world* may be specific to reality therapy, the notion of finding out what the other wants is common to all counseling approaches. Imagine trying to help someone if neither of you had an idea of what it was they wanted! In reality therapy, we talk about *present behaviors,* but all approaches consider, in one way or another, what behaviors the other has already attempted.

It is at the point of self-evaluation that reality therapy distinguishes itself. Most other approaches move from information gathering—"What do you want and what are you doing?"—to analysis and prescription—"This is what I hear you telling me and this is what you ought to do." In the course of this analysis and prescription, we often evaluate for the other person: "You tell me you want to graduate, but you're not doing what you need to do. Let me tell you something, and I'm only telling you this because I care about you, if you don't get down to serious work and change your behavior, you're headed for failure."

The moment we evaluate for others, we lose an opportunity to let them take responsibility for their own lives. Our evaluation is counterproductive for a number of reasons:

- It often invites arguing, as the person tries to justify what has been done.

- Since all behavior is purposeful and represents a best attempt at that moment, people will often try to convince you *why* they have acted the way they have.

- You evaluating their behavior as unsuccessful or ineffective creates an environment in which they feel as if they have no competence (power), at least in that area. This in turn lowers self-esteem and the person interacts with you from a position of weakness.

- Finally, when you evaluate for someone else, you are externalizing the decision-making process. Over time this leads to the development of a world view characterized by irresponsibility and passivity.

It's so tempting and easy to evaluate for someone else. As I stand to the side, I can see things more clearly than you and see what you are doing wrong. I enjoy telling you what you're doing incorrectly or how ineffective your behaviors are because I get to play the role of expert (power) without having to do the difficult work of changing behaviors.

As I listen to people evaluate for others, I am impressed by this fact: frequently, the outside evaluator is *right*. The advice they give, their prescriptions for success are often sound and sensible—"You need to set aside a time every day to do your homework. And remember, homework isn't just written homework. Reviewing your notes and preparing for upcoming tests is just as important." The irony is that their evaluations, advice, and prescriptions are usually unheard or unheeded. People will change only when *they* make the self-evaluation that their current behavior is not taking them in the direction that they want to go.

### Why People Change Their Behavior

When we evaluate for someone else and prescribe behaviors, we are essentially trying to control them and *make* them do something. Usually, we really do believe we are doing it "for their own good," but it still involves an attempt to coerce someone into doing something different. Let's take a few minutes and think about why anyone decides to change. I am taking the position that there is an underlying and identifiable pattern that explains why and how people decide to change behavior. In other words, the process involved when I decide to change my behavior is not unlike the process that you would use when you change your behavior. While the specifics vary depending on the situation, the process is a constant.

Consider the case of the actively drinking alcoholic. We are probably all familiar with cases where loving family members, co-workers, and a host of others have tried to *make* the alcoholic stop drinking. While I am not saying that our efforts are of no value or don't matter, the fact is that the alcoholic will not give up his drinking behaviors until he makes the evaluation that drinking is causing him such problems in his life that he had better find another way. Our efforts are important. Without such loving feedback, often painful to give and to receive, the alcoholic might never change, but our external efforts cannot force another to give up drinking. Those who work with this population talk about the alcoholic "hitting bottom." When the alcoholic "hits bottom" and makes the self-evaluation that drinking is not working, the process of change can begin. Through our efforts we can "raise the bottom" and accelerate the process somewhat, but the alcoholic still needs to "hit bottom." In choice theory terminology, they have to have their scales sufficiently tipped to initiate the change process.

Most of us believe what I have outlined in the last paragraph—that the alcoholic will only stop drinking when he makes that decision. Many of us would go on to say that the self-evaluation alone is not sufficient, but that other help would be required, like counseling or AA. But almost all of us would accept that self-evaluation is a necessary component in the change process. If it is true in the case of alcoholism and the behavior of drinking, I suggest to you that it is equally true in all cases involving behavioral change.

I often wonder why we can accept that the alcoholic needs to self-evaluate before he can change his behavior, yet we continue to try to force others to change without giving them the same opportunity to self-evaluate. For example, we try to "make" students do their homework, study harder, be responsible. We hear endless talk about how to "motivate" others, as if motivation can come from an outside source. As a parent and teacher, I no longer believe I can "make" people do anything or "motivate" them. Instead, it is my responsibility to nurture an environment allowing them to honestly self-evaluate so they take advantage of the internal motivation driving all of us.

Very often I do what other people want me to do. My wife may ask me to do something for her and I comply almost automatically. After awhile, I may come to believe that she "makes" me to certain things but it's never true. I do what I do because I make the evaluation that it is more need-satisfying to do what she asks than to refuse. At that moment, it may be that my need for freedom has been reasonably well-satisfied and doing what my wife has asked gives me an opportunity to satisfy my genetic instruction to be loving. But as habitual as it may be, I behave based upon my internal self-evaluations, not because some outside force makes me.

Take a minute and consider the language of irresponsibility permeating our vocabularies. "I have to get up early tomorrow;" "I have to go to work;" "I don't want to go to this party, but I really need to." Each time we communicate that way, we perpetuate the myth that we are externally controlled. Since so many of us as adults communicate this way, is it any wonder that our children develop irresponsible orientations?

Just for a minute, *really* consider all these "have to, need to" statements we make and check out just how true they are. Do you really *have to* get up early or go to work? Almost assuredly you do not. That's not to say that you should not or that there will be no consequences if you decide not to. Still, such a statement is an exaggeration and a failure to acknowledge that you are making a choice to live your life in a particular way. Acknowledging that you don't *have to* get up early, but that you *choose to* for some very good reasons doesn't mean you will always enjoy getting up early, but it will help you realize that you are an active, rational being who self-evaluates and constantly makes choices about how to best meet your needs at any given time.

Sometimes we choose certain behaviors so regularly that we forget they are choices. They seem to just "happen" to us and we believe they are caused by outside sources. Take the behavior of getting angry, for example. It's not unusual for parents to become angry when their children "misbehave." Before I had comfortably internalized choice theory principles, I would sometimes say, "My son makes me angry when he misbehaves." Angering is not a behavior I am proud of, so I preferred to blame my son (or anyone else) for my anger, rather than take responsibility for it myself. But you know what? My son doesn't make me anything. He doesn't make me angry. He doesn't *make* me happy. All he does, like the rest of us, is *behave.* When he chooses behavior that is different from what I want and what is in my quality world, it's easy for me to identify it as "misbehavior," and tell people he "makes" me angry. When he chooses behaviors that conform to my quality world vision of how a son behaves, it's easy to say he *makes* me happy. In both cases, I am wrong.

**TRY THIS ACTIVITY** Here's an activity for you. If you really want to internalize these principles and not just read about them, pay more attention to your own use of language. Do you say that you believe in freedom and responsibility but use the language of irresponsibility and imprisonment?

- How often do you say you "have to" when you don't?

- How often to you say other people "make" you happy, angry, frustrated, etc.?

- Do you know some people who can really "push your buttons"?

Think of a time when someone insisted that you do something and you refused. It's irrelevant what the situation was or even when you did it. If you can remember just one time when someone insisted that you *had* to do something and you just didn't do it, you have concrete proof that you cannot be *made* to do anything. In that one experience, you made the decision that it was more need-satisfying to behave differently from how you were told you *had* to behave. Every decision you make, large or small, follows the same process. You quickly, often non-consciously, self-evaluate and behave in a way that seems most need-satisfying at that moment.

### Planning New Behaviors

Until a person makes the evaluation that what he is doing is not working well enough for them, there will be no change. You have to stay with that part of the process before you can move on to the planning stage. Why would I even consider planning new behaviors if I haven't determined that my current ones aren't adequate?

If you find that people are unable to make an honest self-evaluation (even when it's painfully obvious to you that their lives are moving in a disastrous direction), it usually is a signal that your involvement is not strong enough.

Over the years, I have learned that people will honestly self-evaluate in environments that are safe and designed to help them move in positive directions. If they believe that the environment is hostile or even neutral they will be less likely to take the risk associated with genuine self-evaluation. In such cases, the protective defense mechanisms they have developed over time prevent them from seeing clearly and evaluating honestly.

Involvement is the key. When I have developed genuine involvement and communicated to the other that "I care about you," they are usually eager to self-evaluate in an honest, genuine way. Involvement is more than communicating, "I won't hurt you." It's communicating, "I'm here to help you and support you in your journey toward quality." In such an environment, virtually all people flourish.

Once the self-evaluation has been made, it is time to begin the process of planning new, more effective, responsible behaviors. This part can be a trap and offers you an opportunity to put your skills into practice. Once a person has acknowledged that their current behaviors are not working well enough, you ask them a question like, "Would you like to try something different?" At this point, remember the reality therapy principle that all people are doing the best they can, especially if you are greeted with anger, sarcasm, or frustration. It is not unusual for the other to say something like, "Don't you think I'd try something else if I could? I don't *know* what else to do?" The unskilled practitioner can easily stumble here. You have worked hard to communicate caring, to help others honestly evaluate the direction in which they are taking their life, and they talk to you *like that?* Righteous indignation may become your choice and you might find yourself saying, "Look, I'm just trying to help *you. Your* the one who has just *admitted* that your life is not going very well. I don't need that kind of treatment. When you decide you want to treat me with the kind of respect all people deserve, I'll be ready to talk with you."

As the lecture continues, all hope of helping and effecting positive change goes out the window. I have seen this happen many times over the years. Well-intentioned, but unskilled people get distracted by the defensive maneuvering and emotionalism of the person they're trying to help. To be successful, you need to be prepared for the emotional behavior you will likely encounter and not let it sidetrack you from your goal—to help people make better choices.

■ **HOW TO HANDLE EMOTIONAL BEHAVIORS** How exactly do you handle the emotional behavior if you encounter it? I like to say something like this:

> It is clear that you are frustrated and I'm sure you've tried everything you could think of up until now. But my question is still the same: 'Would you like to try something else?' If we can figure out something else together that we both agree has a good chance of being more successful, do you want to give it a shot?

I think it's important to acknowledge frustration, anger, or whatever emotion is present. Some practitioners of reality therapy prefer to move right past the negative and begin generating solutions. While I don't want to spend any unnecessary time on negatives, I think it helps build genuine involvement when I acknowledge the negative feeling. Without that acknowledgment, it's easy to believe that reality therapy ignores what is painful. To get beyond the pain to a place where better choices are made, pain has to be acknowledged, not ignored.

■ **BUILDING A PLAN TO CHANGE BEHAVIOR** Building a plan takes some effort. The best plans have the following characteristics: they are short, simple, not contingent upon someone else's behavior, success-oriented, and measurable. Don't be afraid to develop plans that are short and simple. The most important thing about plans is that they are successful. If you develop a plan and the only complaint is that it was "too easy," that's a problem easily rectified. What you don't want is failure. Especially with people who have had a lot of failure in their lives, another failure is the last thing they need. What they need is to be successful in a responsible way, to begin to build a success identity.

**WATCH OUT FOR THESE PEOPLE** Be especially careful with people who have had a long history of failure, are personally unpopular and socially awkward. Quite often, these people have a tendency to develop grandiose plans. They are so thrilled that someone finally has shown some genuine interest in them and given them the hope that they can be successful, that they want desperately not to disappoint. In their desperation, they are likely to promise more than they are capable of delivering. In these cases, I believe our role is to help the other scale the plan down to a more manageable level and maximize the likelihood of success. If we allow another to make a plan that we sincerely believe will result in another failure, we are only perpetuating the failure identity and behaving irresponsibly ourselves.

**AVOID PLANS THAT RELY ON OTHERS** Whenever possible, try to make plans that do not rely on the behavior of someone else. If I commit to doing something *as long as someone else does this or that,* I have given up my power and autonomy. If the other doesn't come through, I have a built-in excuse for my failure. In reality therapy we try to help people behave in successful, responsible ways *regardless of what others do.* Even if the plan is successful, if it is contingent upon the behavior of another, it perpetuates the belief system that my success or failure is due to other people and forces over which I have no control. It supports the posture of helpless victimization we are trying to overcome. I would rather develop a more modest plan that relies on no one but the individual than a more elaborate plan that requires the efforts of another. (By the way, this is not to suggest that we don't need one another. I believe we do. Interdependence is greater than independence. Still, the pathway of responsibility requires that I learn how to act in a responsible way regardless of what those around me choose to do.)

**WHO MAKES THE PLAN?** I have a rule of thumb when I am working with anyone, regardless of their age or ability: I give as little help as possible and as much as necessary. Ideally, the plan should come from the other. Frequently, however, the other person needs some help. Help may take the form of brainstorming ideas or may be more directive. A number of my colleagues in reality therapy insist that the plan be made by the other. I am somewhat less ambitious, although I first try to attain that ideal. I look at it this way. There are certain things I just don't know. Information I have no access to on my own. If you ask me to generate solutions in areas where I am essentially ignorant, or at least ineffective, we won't end up with something that reflects quality. If, on the other hand, you can provide me with information and ideas, I have more raw material to work with and I'll likely end up with something better than I would have if I had been left to my own devices. The same is true in planning. Let's pretend I am working with a student and I have information that would be helpful to her as she makes her plans. I believe it would be irresponsible on my part to withhold that information. My role is to give her access to as much relevant information as possible so she can make the best possible decision.

Sometimes you will work with people who are simply less creative or resourceful at that particular point in time, or who for some other reason can't develop a plan independently. Under those conditions, I am comfortable brainstorming, creating several possibilities to choose from as they develop their plan. By creating options, you still encourage the other to decide, a key component in developing a sense of personal responsibility. On the other hand, if you simply make a suggestion, the other person may experience momentary success but they will not develop responsibility.

Whenever possible, make some kind of contingency plan. "What will you do if...?" is a good question that promotes thinking and helps people respect the idea that sometimes things don't go as we plan. The key is how we handle things when they don't go the way we hoped or expected. Creating contingency plans helps in that regard.

**GETTING A COMMITMENT**  It's helpful for you and the other person to have a sense of how badly they want something. The level of commitment may vary and indicates how serious the person is about wanting to change the direction of their life.

I worked with a student a few years ago who was in danger of failing most of his seventh grade classes and being retained. Everyone involved, from teachers to parents to the student himself, agreed that he was capable of doing the required work. As we worked together, I helped this student identify just how committed he was to earning promotion to the eighth grade. Superficially, he wanted to be promoted. When I asked him the simple question, "Do you want to be in the eighth grade next year?" he had no trouble answering in the affirmative. In fact, he laughed at the absurdity of the question. "Of course I want to be in the eighth grade next year," he told me. "How badly do you want it?" I asked. He seemed confused by the question and asked me exactly what I meant. "Well," I said, "let me give you an example. Like lots of other adults, I wouldn't mind having more money. So if you asked me if I would like to be rich, I'd probably say 'Yes.' But if you asked me if I would be willing to work a second job or switch to a job that pays more, I'm not so sure I'd be interested. It all depends on how much you want something. Do you want it enough to just think about it or are you willing to do something about it? And if you are willing to do something about it, exactly what are you willing to do?"

He understood and we were then able to figure out just how committed he was to reaching the eighth grade. He determined that he was willing to do one extra hour of work every school day for the last three months of school in order to earn promotion. I asked him if he believed that would be enough work to attain his goal, another evaluation question. Because we had developed enough of a genuine involvement, he was honest with me and said, "Probably not" and we moved on. We finally agreed that doing two hours extra work for the next three months would probably lead to success. This led me to ask, "Are you willing to commit to doing two additional hours work each night for the next three months in order to get what you want?" I know what answer *I* wanted. *He* knew what answer I wanted. Fortunately, we had enough respect for each other that we spoke the truth and didn't settle for socially expected and desired answers. He told me he would not commit to two hours extra work every night. Regardless of what happened with this student, I am convinced he learned more about himself and more about taking responsibility for your own life through our interactions than he would have if we had acted differently toward each other.

WRITTEN CONTRACTS  Relative to commitments, I am sometimes asked how I feel about written contracts. I used to answer that question by saying that I don't like contracts, that they seem too much like a behavior modification strategy, and I prefer a handshake and verbal commitment. Recently, however, I have changed my thinking. I have more closely examined my role and my goal. What I discovered was this: *my* feelings about written contracts are essentially irrelevant. My goal is to be helpful to some other person and if I want to be as successful as possible, I need to develop flexibility and find out what the other person wants and needs from me. More and more, I find myself asking the others what *they* need. If a written contract is something they perceive to be helpful, then we develop one. If a written contract is not going to help them, we figure out another way to make sure there is a strong commitment to the plan.

FOLLOWING UP  Finally, once a plan is committed to, you need to have some type of follow-up to check on how successful the plan is. The follow-up maintains and enhances the involvement, communicating to the other, "I care enough about you to re-establish contact and find out if you followed through on your plan." The follow-up session provides another opportunity to let the other self-evaluate and grow in responsibility. It may be tempting to reward and punish, depending on how successful the other was. Try to give up these familiar but unhelpful behaviors and give the others a chance to evaluate their own behaviors. For example, let's pretend a student told you she was going to complete all assigned written homework. When you see her, she shows you the work, neatly done and complete. The traditional, common sense, S-R way of dealing with that situation is to praise the student for doing what she said she would do. Praise feels good but it is not as valuable as self-evaluation if you are trying to help people develop a sense of responsibility.

When I am in a situation like this, I now ask, "What do you think about that?" This gives the students a chance to publicly take responsibility and articulate that they feel good about themselves for having behaved in a responsible way. I will then affirm what the students have said but I always ask them to self-evaluate before I comment.

When students fails to do what was planned, it is important not to punish them. Punishing them only compromises whatever involvement you have developed and minimizes the chance of future success. Instead, calmly say something like this: "When we spoke last time, this plan seemed like a good idea. Does it still seem worthwhile to you or not?" Assuming it does, I will say, "OK, if it's still a good idea, let's figure out a better plan, one that will work." Then you go about the business of building a better plan. Blaming, guilting, and punishing only wastes time. If the plan no longer seems like a good idea, revise it.

The process of reality therapy never really ends, in part, because it is not simply a counseling process. It is a way of interacting with others and operationalizing the principles of choice theory. It gives us a way to be with each other in a way which helps us each identify our wants, what we've done to be successful, and to evaluate our behavior. From there, we can make plans to continue our success or plan new more effective strategies. As teachers working with students, we can utilize this process every day, making a reality therapy orientation very practical and usable. Academically and socially, we can help students identify their wants. Furthermore, we can help them expand their quality world so that working hard academically and behaving in pro-social ways becomes a part of their quality world. From there we can utilize the rest of the process of reality therapy to build the kinds of schools we have in our quality worlds.

# CHAPTER 4

# *An Introduction to Quality Schools*

Choice theory is the theoretical foundation underlying everything presented in this book. Reality therapy is a process allowing choice theory principles to be operationalized. Quality schools represent the application of choice theory and reality therapy ideas to education. Dr. Glasser has written extensively about quality schools and I encourage you to read both *The Quality School* and *The Quality School Teacher*. In this section, I provide you with a summary of what I consider to be the most essential elements of a quality school. As you continue your journey toward quality you can fill in specifics, but this should provide you with sufficient information to make a good start.

The quality school movement developed by Dr. Glasser is built upon the work of W. Edwards Deming, a noted industrialist. Deming was considered by many to have been the most influential individual in the Japanese rise to economic power after World War II. At that time, the Japanese had a reputation for low-quality workmanship. Deming convinced them that if they listened to his ideas, he would teach them how to create quality products that the world would want to buy. The Japanese listened.

Deming's ideas are geared toward the workplace. Glasser has taken these notions and applied them to schools. Glasser streamlined Deming's complex system of 14 principles and seven deadly sins to three essential elements. These three elements form the heart and soul of a quality school:

1. Eliminate coercion

2. Focus on quality

3. Institute a system of self-evaluation

In practice, each school pursuing increased quality will be unique. What is most appropriate in one setting may be less ideal in another. It is for that reason that there is no recipe for a quality school. If there were, quality could be achieved by copying the best models available. That approach will not yield true quality, however, for real quality is only realized when a school's uniqueness serves as the foundation upon which quality principles are constructed. While there is much to be gained by visiting especially strong schools, don't think you can mimic them and capture the quality they have achieved. A major component in the quest for quality is the journey itself, and there are no shortcuts when you decide to take the journey to quality.

Even though each quality school will be different from all others, there are certain core characteristics common among the quality schools that implement the ideas advocated by Dr. Glasser. They all work to eliminate coercion, focus upon quality work, and utilize the process of self-evaluation.

## ELIMINATE COERCION

Currently our schools are highly coercive institutions. In nearly every relationship imaginable, coercion is present: teacher to student, student to student, teacher to teacher, administrator to teacher, etc. From a choice theory standpoint, the problem with coercion is easy to identify. When you coerce me, it is difficult for me to follow my genetic instructions to be powerful and free. Frequently I choose to resent you for this, frustrating my instruction to be loving. Not surprisingly, in such an environment there is little fun. The coercive environment is decidedly unsatisfying and in such an environment quality work is almost never done.

On a purely theoretical level, it is impossible to coerce anybody. As my children are quick to remind me, nobody can *make* you do anything. Crusaders, hunger-strikers, and others who are willing to sacrifice their lives for any cause to which they're committed prove this to be true. On a practical level, however, people *do* coerce each other. You have power over me and use coercive behaviors to get me to do something. While I may be able to choose to defy you in theory, I realize that it would be unwise to do so. I conform and do what you ask, but because my needs have been frustrated, I generally do *just enough to get you off my back*. My agenda becomes wonderfully simple and focused—do enough to get you to leave me alone. Even if I *do* end up performing quality work, it is not because you coerced me. Your coercion will lead, at best, to compliance. I will only consciously attempt do quality work when I believe doing so will satisfy me and add quality to my life.

*Eliminate coercion.* I don't know about you, but that sounds like a massive undertaking to me. When we practice reality therapy, we are careful to develop plans that are success-oriented. It is more effective to successfully take a first step than to attempt to do too much and fail. I urge you to keep this notion in mind as you work to eliminate coercion. If your school is like most, coercion is currently widely used and in many ways it holds the school together. To impulsively eliminate it without having something better to put in its place would be counterproductive.

I have worked with schools that have made this mistake. Their intentions were noble and they worked diligently to eliminate coercion. Unfortunately, they moved too quickly before figuring out what to use instead of coercion. In a nutshell, here's what happened:

- The day-to-day coercive behaviors used by classroom teachers were abandoned. With no effective substitute in place, discipline problems increased both in frequency and intensity.

- As the situation worsened, administrators, deans of students, and others in the role of maintaining appropriate behavior in the school grew increasingly frustrated.

- As their scales became more and more tipped, they considered all the behaviors available to them to move the school into line with the quality world vision they held dear. Despite their philosophical opposition to coercion, they had no other more effective behaviors to use.

- Not surprisingly, they reluctantly returned to the coercive patterns of behavior they had known and used for years. Because discipline problems had worsened, they coerced with increased vigor, even more frustrated than they had been in the past because they had been "nice guys" who were "taken advantage of" by the "unruly students." Ironically, the attempt to eliminate coercion led to an even more coercive environment.

- Just as importantly, the students began to trust the teachers and administrators less. They believed that "eliminate coercion" was just a hollow phrase. They were convinced that the school was more coercive than ever and school officials were not to be trusted.

If you move too quickly in this area, you will likely fail and end up with a more coercive environment in the long run. As much as I want to eliminate coercion, I caution you to move very slowly. In fact, I would suggest that you would be better served by focusing your energy in other areas. Specifically, work to make classrooms more need-satisfying to both students and teachers and you will find there is less and less "misbehavior" and fewer instances when coercion is even considered. When students can meet their needs by working toward quality academic standards they do not need to be coerced. They will quite naturally do what you ask because in doing so they are able to follow the instructions built into their genetic structure. "We can't just let kids do what they want," I am frequently reminded, usually by a highly-committed, passionate teacher who is frustrated and confused by my "liberal" approach. While I am a strong proponent of structure and appreciate the need to have well-ordered classrooms, I find this comment interesting. Once we help students perceive the value of learning what we are trying to teach and once they have put the curriculum into their quality worlds, then we certainly *can* let students do what they want.

### Consider Why We Use Coercion

To prevent an impulsive "let's get rid of all coercion immediately" mentality and to move toward a more sensible approach to education reform, let's take a look at coercion from a choice theory perspective.

Remember: *all behavior is purposeful*. That includes even less ideal behaviors like coercing others. If coercing is purposeful, what is its intent? Almost always, it is to get someone else to do what you want them to do. As teachers, there are lots of things we believe the students need to do. That's part of our role. So the intent behind coercing is not inherently at odds with our role as teachers. If the goal or intent is consistent with our role, the problem is the behavior of coercing itself. It develops an atmosphere that is not need-satisfying and does not lead to quality. Let me use choice theory language to clarify what I mean. There is not necessarily anything flawed with what I want (quality world level). The failure comes with the coercive behaviors I use (present behaviors).

To help you become more successful in your goal to eliminate coercion, I suggest that you give up the struggle to *eliminate* coercion. Instead of focusing on that far-away, ideal place, focus your energy in an area where you can experience success *now*. Take some time and think of just a few situations when you currently coerce others where you could behave less coercively and still get what you want from the situation. Begin there and don't push yourself any further. If you are willing to commit to a course of action, you can begin the process of eliminating coercion *now*.

Remember to choose situations that you can give up the coercion without sacrificing your effectiveness. Coercion is purposeful and if you eliminate it *and* give up your effectiveness, you will quickly become frustrated and go back to coercion in a hurry and probably with increased energy. If you can give up the coercive behaviors *without* sacrificing your effectiveness, you will begin to shed the shackles of your coercion easily. You will literally feel lighter as you discover ways to be effective without resorting to coercive behaviors.

As you begin to experience success, your creativity will offer you additional ideas about where you can give up more and more coercion. If you are fortunate enough to be working with colleagues interested in the same journey, you can swap ideas and strategies about how to minimize your coercive behaviors and increase your effectiveness as a manager.

Over time, coercion will gradually fall away and become less of an issue in your classroom and school. Will we ever totally eliminate coercion? I'm not sure, but there's so much of it now that the question has little practical value. It is interesting to note that Deming did not mention coercion per se. He phrased it this way: *Drive fear out of the work place.* Because I find so many of us have different perceptions about what is or what is not coercion, I prefer Deming's phrasing. You may be unclear about whether something is coercive, but you can usually identify if there is fear in an environment, at least for yourself. Consider the following questions with this concept in mind:

- In your school, is there fear?
- Do the students fear you?
- Do you fear some of your colleagues?
- Do teachers fear the administrators?
- Do administrators fear the teachers?
- Do teachers fear the parents?
- Do parents fear school personnel?

If you answer "yes" to any of these, you have a place to begin working. Start building an environment where fear has been driven out. In a fear-driven system, mediocrity rules. In a system where fear has been eliminated, quality has a chance to flourish.

I want to make a final point about minimizing coercion and driving fear out of our schools. We need to minimize coercion in *all* relationships, not just teacher to student. As I work with teachers from around the country, the ones who are most frustrated are the ones who feel as if choice theory and quality school ideas are being *forced* upon them but not practiced by those above them. Paradoxically, they believe they are being coerced into giving up coercion while they continue to be subjected to coercion by those with power over them. This creates one of the least satisfying atmospheres possible in which to work. Because the environment is so difficult, teachers in these schools spend much of their professional energy just trying to survive. There may be lots of superficial conversation about quality, but there is very little in action.

To minimize coercion, we need to move from traditional "boss management" to what is called "lead management."

## Boss Management

Systems traditionally have relied upon a system of management best described as "boss management." This approach is built upon a hierarchy. Bosses are listened to and obeyed because they have power over their subordinates. They capitalize on the fear that exists in the workplace and coerce workers into doing what is expected of them. Most schools operate from a boss management perspective. Within the building, teachers do what the principal says because to do otherwise is to risk painful consequences. In an extreme case, a teacher may lose a job. In less extreme but more numerous cases, teachers conform because to defy the boss may mean a less favorable class schedule, a particularly difficult class, or an especially unattractive room. In such schools teachers may fear negative evaluations, so they grudgingly conform, operating on a survival level much of the time. While the picture I have painted may seem extreme, I have heard stories like this from teachers in schools around the country.

Principals not only boss, they generally are bossed from above. The superintendent may use the same coercive behaviors with the principals with essentially the same results.

Bossing exists in other relationships around the school. Teachers boss their students. Not surprisingly, the students don't like it any better than the teachers do. Most of them conform, threatened by poor grades, phone calls home, detention, suspension, and humiliation in front of their peers. But don't confuse conformity with quality.

Bossing generally leads to conformity. In certain systems, conformity may be an appropriate goal and bossing may be the way to go. I don't want to suggest that bossing is *always* wrong and that systems that need only compliance in order to prosper cannot successfully utilize a boss-managed approach. The question really comes down to the mission of the system in question. As educators, we claim to want to pursue quality. If that is really true and not simply a meaningless platitude, bossing won't work. In order to achieve quality, boss management must give way to lead management.

## Lead Management

The lead manager differs from the boss manager in several ways. Whereas a boss tells you what to do, a leader will show you. The boss is more intent on assessing blame and controlling things by rewarding good workers and punishing poor workers. The leader, on the other hand, helps each worker contribute as much as possible and is primarily interested in helping the organization pursue quality. Leaders make it clear that their job is to help the workers do their jobs better, to teach them new, helpful skills, to help them become more competent and more valuable to the organization.

Contrary to some beliefs, effective lead managers do not "water down" standards and settle for the least common denominator. Those who are seeking to move toward lead management frequently confuse lead management with a lack of vision. In fact, the lead managers who are most successful are true visionaries. They have a clear sense of where they want to take a school and how a quality school would operate. Their skill is that they are able to engage as many of the staff and as much of the community as possible—including the students—to collectively forge a clear vision of quality. Successful lead managers are able to reach out to virtually everyone and communicate to them the following message:

- We are stronger and more capable with your input.

- Your ideas are valued, even though we will not always move in the direction you suggest.

- We want you to continue to think about ways in which we can make this school even better.

- Your ideas will always be listened to and taken seriously.

Finally, effective lead managers have tremendous energy and are able to help others find energy as well.

Less skilled lead managers are often tentative and too cautious. Fearful of offending others, they fail to lead, to articulate a vision of a quality school. They try endlessly to build coalitions and reach compromise so that there are no hurt feelings. The result is a school that is always treading water. With various interest groups within the school and community competing, the lead manager scrambles, attempting to placate this group and that. The school does not appear to change much from year to year, but it is not a healthy conservatism that comes from honest self-evaluation and a desire to progress slowly and wisely. It is an uneasy conservativism, fueled by the failure to take a stand and move toward increased quality. Over time, people in these systems lose energy and enthusiasm. The school turns into a deadly place in which to work instead of being vital, evolving, and constantly improving.

A lead management approach by everyone involved in managing (teachers, building administrators, central office administrators, school boards) will help minimize the coercive behaviors that currently dominate and make it difficult to successfully pursue quality.

## FOCUS ON QUALITY

In a quality school, the emphasis is always on the quality of the work done or the quality of the interaction among people. Quantity takes a back seat.

Currently, many teachers are hampered by curriculum demands that dictate *how much* is to be covered during the school year. Even if significant numbers of students have not mastered a given concept, teachers feel compelled to move quickly through the curriculum because there is an expectation that a certain number of chapters must be *covered* during the course of the year. This, in fact, is exactly what happens. A certain number of chapters are covered. This does not mean that the material presented in those chapters has been addressed in a quality fashion and the concepts have been mastered by the students.

In a quality school, fewer concepts are presented. Fewer chapters are covered, but more are mastered. Since the emphasis is on quality, students are expected to improve their performance until they have at least demonstrated mastery (often seen as achieving at an 80 percent level or better.) Students who have not demonstrated this level of achievement continue to work until they have mastered what is being presented.

Teachers who are unfamiliar with these practices frequently find it difficult to believe that students will continue to work in an effort to improve the quality of their work. They are used to more traditional schools where students turn in work, have it evaluated by teachers, and a new concept is then introduced. In such settings, the evaluation process serves to identify the "winners" and "losers," a largely irrelevant process since most teachers know before any formal assessment which students will be successful and which students are not yet ready to demonstrate mastery. There will be certain cases where more time and effort will not result in mastery as it is typically defined. Students with cognitive deficits, developmental delays, learning disabilities, or other handicapping conditions may need to have expectations modified. Still, these students represent the minority, and deserve the same opportunity to demonstrate what is quality for them.

Clearly identifying a person's job or role can make teaching easier. The job is intimately connected to the mission and is a clear, unambiguous description of what is to be done.

I regularly tell my own children that their job in school is to learn as much as possible. It's that simple. I am not particularly concerned with the grade they receive, in part because all grading is somewhat subjective and arbitrary. By helping my children clearly identify their job as students, they can more easily identify and choose the behaviors that appropriately match their job.

The same is true for teachers. I believe that our job is to teach students the best way we know how. Anything we do should be consistent with that. Whatever we do that conflicts with our primary role—teaching—needs to be evaluated, modified, and perhaps abandoned. I will address this issue more fully when discussing the issue of grading and report cards.

### Defining Quality Work

How exactly can we define quality work? Dr. Albert Mamary, former Superintendent of chools in Johnson City, New York, a system often cited when quality schools are discussed, defines quality work as the best that a student can do *at this time*. The phrase *at this time* is critically important because it acknowledges that a host of variables are involved which impact quality of work. The concept of quality school work has several components which are important.

■ **BEST EFFORT**  Quality represents my best effort.

■ **CONTINUOUS IMPROVEMENT**  The concept of quality includes the notion of continuous improvement. There is almost no job that cannot be improved upon and quality seeks to constantly improve. I remember one time reading an interview with John Lennon. When the interviewer asked Lennon if there were any Beatle songs he would do differently if he could, Lennon laughed and said, "All of them!" Even though many Beatle songs are considered to be quality by millions, Lennon recognized that even quality work can be improved.

■ **ITS USEFUL**  Quality work is useful. That does not mean it needs to be utilitarian, although it can be. A work of art, a poem, is useful because it adds beauty and joy to the world.

One of our jobs is to help students understand *why* what we are asking them to do is worth doing and worth doing well. Perhaps some of us were brought up in a time when adults didn't need to explain this to students. Like it or not, however, those days are gone. Many students today want to know *why* before they will expend significant energy. Since quality work requires commitment and energy, we will be better off if we provide them the information they need to appreciate the relevance of what we are asking them to do.

■ **IT FEELS GOOD** Quality work always feels good because in doing it we are satisfying our needs and following our genetic instructions particularly the need for power and competence. Think of things you have accomplished in your life, professionally or personally, which you would identify as high quality. As you reflect upon these things, you are probably flooded with powerful good feelings. You probably worked hard. You may have sacrificed. There may have been pain involved. But when all is said and done, these situations felt good because they added quality to your life. You became a stronger person by having experienced them.

■ **IT'S NEVER DESTRUCTIVE** Reality therapy believes strongly in the concept of responsible behavior. Behaving responsibly means that I cannot satisfy my needs at the expense of another, so quality is never hurtful or destructive.

■ **FLEXIBILITY** In a quality school, as we focus on quality we strive to be as flexible as possible. There would be a number of ways to demonstrate mastery of subject matter. More and more schools are working with alternative assessment techniques. What is frequently referred to as "authentic assessment" is gaining popularity and is consistent with the quality school concept of relevance.

Almost 20 years ago, before I was well versed in reality therapy and before Dr. Glasser wrote about choice theory, I had a chance to help draft our school's philosophy as we were preparing for the accrediting process. One of our opening statements captures a central concept that would be present in my vision of a quality school. We said that our role was to meet all students where they were and to bring them as far as they could go. There is no doubt that we work with students of widely varying abilities. With an increased emphasis on including special needs students in mainstreamed classes, the diversity will increase. None of these factors should impact one of our central missions in a quality school:

*To accept students where they currently are and to teach them as much as possible in the time we are together.*

By utilizing the process of reality therapy and creating need-satisfying classrooms and schools, we can fulfill our missions.

■ **TIME** Since our primary concern in a quality school is quality work, time is a less important factor. For example, if a test were given in a quality school and a student did not finish during class, he would be encouraged to take extra time in order to complete the test to the best of his ability. Too often today, students who know a great deal are penalized because they do not finish an exam in a prescribed period of time. Although there may be some cases where speed is a critically important factor, generally this is not so. If a student takes his time, organizes slowly, offers complete information to the questions asked, and needs additional time, it should be provided without question and without penalty. The requirement to finish within a prescribed time period is counter to my vision of quality. It also teaches students that the skill most prized in schools is to quickly summarize important facts. While this is undoubtedly a valuable skill that I believe should be taught, it is given more weight than other, equally important issues like depth of thought and thoughtful reflection.

## SELF-EVALUATION/CONCURRENT EVALUATION

The third common denominator among quality schools is a belief in self-evaluation and concurrent evaluation. In traditional boss-managed schools, evaluation is almost always a top-down affair. Superiors evaluate inferiors and judge their work, issuing a grade or some other evaluative device. Most of us work in schools like this. As classroom teachers, we grade the students; they are not asked to evaluate their work, at least not in any meaningful way. We, too, are evaluated by our administrators. Again, they may solicit our comments about how *we* think we are doing our jobs, but we all know that we are evaluated by the administrator and our comments are only a minor part of the process. In most settings, principals, as well, are evaluated from above by a central office administrator using the same boss-manager, top-down approach.

Identifying the flaw in such an arrangement is easy if looked at through a choice theory lens. Choice theorists believe that self-evaluation is essential to initiate meaningful change leading in the direction of increased quality. Traditional evaluation is external. You are evaluated by an outside agent. Because this outside agent often has legitimate authority over you (i.e. the power to give you a poor grade, the power to give you a poor evaluation, the power to dismiss you from a job), the need for survival is threatened and our behavior is designed to restore balance by behaving in ways to ensure our survival. For most of us this means we choose behaviors that the boss advocates. We are not driven by the boss' picture of quality. Rather, we are driven by our own need to survive. In such cases we generally do enough to ensure survival, but we are almost never concerned about doing quality work.

As we begin to behave in ways that increase the chances of survival (i.e. passing a course, getting an acceptable evaluation, etc.), an interesting phenomenon occurs. While we have been successfully behaving in a way that increases our chance of surviving, our behavior is contrary to our genetic instruction to be free. This internal system of checks and balances leads us to conform enough to survive but to rebel enough to maintain our freedom, dignity, and self-esteem. The natural extension of this process is that work generally gets done, but quality work is rarely done.

In some cases, even compliance is not achieved. Some individuals have a stronger need for freedom than others and, therefore, have more difficulty doing what they are told to do, even if it is "for their own good." People in this category are likely to have many conflicts with boss managers and do very poorly in systems based upon external evaluation.

## Self-Evaluation

The only time you can be reasonably assured that someone will put forth the effort and energy required to do quality work is when they have had a chance to self-evaluate and have determined that behaving in a particular way will add quality to their lives. This choice theory premise is what is behind the emphasis on building conscious self-evaluation into a quality school. Put simply: any system working with humans ought to be run in a way compatible with how human beings are genetically structured.

What does self-evaluation actually look like when put into place in a quality school? Most obviously, students would now be asked to evaluate the quality of their own work rather than simply turning it in to the teacher. Turning it in to another to be evaluated without first self-evaluating builds an external locus of control and promotes irresponsibility. Instead, we will ask students to evaluate their own efforts first. Once they have determined that their work represents their best effort, what is quality *for them at that time,* it is then turned into the teacher for additional evaluation and feedback.

---

### Concurrent Evaluation

At this point, it is important to introduce the necessary partner of self-evaluation: concurrent evaluation. Pure self-evaluation is limited, especially in a school setting. It is too easy to imagine the following scene: You ask a student to evaluate her own work before turning it in to you. The student is a serious student and wants to do well. Like everyone else, her perception is limited by what she knows. Having been given no model of quality against which to compare her efforts, she is left to her own devices to figure out if her work is ready to be given to you. With the limited information available to her, the student self-evaluates, but in a way which does not necessarily lead to increased quality. As the teacher, you receive the student's paper and grow even more frustrated that the student would pass in something so obviously (to you) lacking in quality.

Returning to a central theme of reality therapy, responsibility, we are faced with this issue: if you ask a student to engage in self-evaluation and do not provide them with the tools necessary to self-evaluate in a productive way, are *you* behaving responsibly?

There is a way to avoid this problem: before having students work independently and evaluate their own work, discuss with them what a quality piece of work would look like.

For example, let's assume you were helping the students write a persuasive paragraph. You might lead a discussion where students discover that the following elements are part of a piece of quality writing: a clear beginning, middle, and end; sufficient supporting arguments to convince a reader; use of vivid language, with examples of what that might look like in print; a paragraph with complete sentences and appropriate transitional devices; and correct spelling and punctuation. What you help the class do is to develop a shared quality world picture of a persuasive paragraph. Now when students are asked to self-evaluate, they have a concrete standard against which they can measure their work.

If students are helping each other edit papers, the specifics will help the editors know what to look for to help their peers improve the quality of what is produced. Students will now be equipped to engage in meaningful, productive self-evaluation and not the superficial self-evaluation that is an enemy to quality school work. In such a model, teachers remain responsible for leading discussions about quality. The quality classroom is far from loose and without definition. Indeed, the vision of high quality academic work is very specific. Remember one of the primary roles of the teacher is to lead students to a greater and richer understanding of what represents quality academic work for them at this point in their educational journey.

When the concept of self-evaluation is fully explained with the notion of concurrent evaluation incorporated, teachers generally embrace it. When I introduce these ideas in a workshop, I generally structure them in such a way that the teachers become quite comfortable with the notion of self-evaluation. By the time this concept is introduced, the teachers have a reasonably good understanding of choice theory. They have decided that the ideas make sense, including the choice theory principle of self-evaluation being a necessary component in the change process. It is easy for them to understand how this can be applied to classroom situations.

Everything goes along wonderfully until I remind them that the three common elements in a quality school are highly integrated and interdependent. This means that genuine self-evaluation will only occur in an environment where coercion has been virtually eliminated and fear has all but disappeared. I offer the following specific examples to help illustrate how this works.

Like most of you, I am evaluated by an administrator in my district. For years I received evaluations which were both very positive and essentially useless in helping me grow professionally. Please don't think for a minute that I complained when I received positive evaluations. Like most of us, I appreciated them. They felt good. It's just that they had virtually nothing to do with any professional growth and development. Several years ago, one of my administrators surprised me when he announced that he was planning to handle the evaluation process differently. "Bob," he said, "this year I am going to leave you a blank evaluation form. I want you to take some time and fill it out in the next week or so. I'll set up a time when we can talk, compare notes, and discuss how things are going." It was an amazing moment for me. Instead of talking *about* self-evaluation, I was suddenly in the midst of it.

### Self-Evaluation And the Fear Factor

It was at that moment that I fully realized that genuine self-evaluation will only occur in an environment which is free of fear. Assume that I respect my administrator and truly believe that his goal is to help me become more skilled and competent as a school psychologist. Seeing him as a facilitator to my growth and someone whom I do not fear, I will much more likely self-evaluate in an honest way because I operate with the belief system that *he is there to help me.* Under these conditions I might say something like, "I think there are a number of areas where I do well, some especially so. But there's one particular area where I know I could probably improve my performance. I write a lot of psychological reports and sometimes I think I might make them a little too jargon-heavy and less helpful to parents than they could be." I engage in this honest self-evaluation because I believe my administrator is there to help me figure out a better way to do my job. I don't fear him, but trust that he can help me grow professionally.

Change the situation for just a moment. This may be more familiar to some of you. Let's pretend that I fear my administrator. He has portrayed himself as "the boss" and made "the bottom line" clear on numerous occasions. We both know that there is a glut of teachers, and while I might be respected, it is well known that like all teachers I am "easily replaced." The same scenario is played out and I am asked to self-evaluate. Do you think for a minute that under those circumstances I will *honestly* self-evaluate my performance as a school psychologist and share that self-evaluation openly? There's almost no chance because I will automatically self-evaluate in a more global way. I will quickly, perhaps non-consciously evaluate the situation and realize that any "admission" of weakness will be used by "them" as "ammunition" to "build a case" against me. The need for survival (retaining my job) takes precedence at that moment, rather than the need for power (increased professional competence) and I conduct myself accordingly. "You know, I've given a lot of thought about this, and I really haven't been able to identify any areas where I'm particularly weak. Like all of us, I imagine I could improve, but nothing jumps out as being a serious weakness. Of course, if there's any area you'd like me to work on, I'd be glad to do my best." Ughh!

When I relate these scenarios to teachers, they almost all immediately understand the critical connection between self-evaluation and the elimination of fear. Along with that realization, there is generally a fair amount of squirming and other displays of discomfort. The participants *really* understand that their classrooms are characterized by coercion and fear. When we talk about it in more general terms, it is easy to pretend that coercion and fear exist *somewhere,* but not in *my room.* Suddenly, they hold up the mirror and do not always like what they see.

Ask yourself this question: Would students engage in honest self-evaluation of their academic efforts in your classroom or are they more likely to avoid such a risky behavior? Many of you may find the courage to acknowledge a painful truth. Too many students would not share any honest self-evaluation because they fear how you will treat them. If you are one of these teachers, you may begin to use the process of reality therapy in a very significant way, starting right now. This isn't just philosophy. This isn't just talk. This is relevant and concerns the kind of teacher you want to be.

If your classroom is characterized by too much fear to allow for open, honest self-evaluation, what can you begin to do now to move it in the direction you wish to go?

Administrators, too, are invited to take a long look in the mirror. If you are in the position of evaluating others, how would they behave if you were to ask them to self-evaluate? Do they see you as a coach who is there to help them become more skilled in their job? Do they see you as someone to be feared, to get past, someone largely disconnected from their professional growth and development? How do you want to be seen by your staff? How will you behave to create an environment where more genuine, meaningful self-evaluation can flourish?

These are not easy questions and deserve your serious consideration. I invite you to share your ideas with colleagues you trust.

## THE ESSENCE OF QUALITY SCHOOLS

Each quality school will be different. Just as each practitioner of reality therapy retains her own unique style, each quality school and quality classroom reflects diversity and uniqueness. Despite their many differences, however, all quality schools will be characterized by the three variables that have been outlined here:

1. an attempt to minimize coercion and drive fear out of the school;

2. a focus on quality work and quality relationships;

3. and the overt and systematic use of self-evaluation and concurrent evaluation by everybody within the school community.

Supported by this foundation, each school can develop its unique vision of quality, a vision that is appropriate to the students and community it serves.

# PART II

# *Inspiring Quality— Practice*

# CHAPTER 5

# *What Do You Want ?*

I am frequently asked who is the most important person when building a quality school. While Glasser has emphasized the importance of the principal in this process, I suggest that the most important person in inspiring quality in your school is *YOU*.

Unless you are the principal, it is a trap to identify the principal as the key person. It automatically shifts the focus away from you and onto someone else. Every time we do that, we abdicate our responsibility and give away our personal power. We put ourselves in the position of passive subservience, waiting for someone else to lead the way. While I will not deny the important role of the building principal in creating a quality school, you are the most important person regardless of your identified role.

Please understand that I am not suggesting that anyone take on a role that is not theirs. I am not advocating violating an established chain of command or suggesting that you work at cross purposes with your administrators. What I am proposing is that you actively work toward inspiring quality in your school in a way consistent with your role in the building. Don't take the less responsible, passive position of waiting for someone else to initiate the dialogue. Do what you can do.

So what can you do and when can you do it? Ironically, it is best to begin by slowing down and taking the symbolic deep breath. If you want to get anywhere, first you better figure out where you want to go. For our purposes, this means you need to develop your own notion of what makes up quality school and how you would conduct yourself in such an environment. This is a tricky and dangerous part of your journey. There are times when we are better off with a highly detailed map. At other times, something a bit sketchy will be more effective. At this point, what you really need is a compass more than a detailed map. You need something to point you in the right direction. A detailed map might do more harm than good. Let me explain.

If there are a number of us who want to take this journey and we all use a compass, we can all agree to move forward in a similar direction. Sometime further along with more information and a greater understanding of where we want to go, we can pool our resources and continue forward together. With personal relationships strengthened over time and the increased appreciation for each other that develops when we have struggled for something valuable together, we can figure out how to continue to move forward as a group. Each individual intentionally remaining less focused increases the chance of the group ultimately embracing a more highly-defined, specific goal. On the other hand, if each of us begins with a highly-defined, detailed map that not only gives us a general direction, but a specific destination, we may never meet another soul along the way. That isolated pathway will not inspire quality in your school because a quality school can only be pursued by a group slowly developing a shared vision.

So how do you proceed? While I can't provide just one answer, I can offer you some suggestions. As you evaluate my ideas, you should judge whether or not they make sense for you. First, you should develop your own vision of a quality school. Second, you should determine how you would behave in that idealized environment.

As you develop your idea of what makes up a quality school think in generalities. In the beginning, specifics will only make building a quality school more difficult; you will be better off establishing the broad parameters of a quality school. When you consider how you would conduct yourself in a quality school, become more specific. You need to ask yourself some very basic questions about what it means to be an educator. Some of you may find it more comfortable to do the intellectual work of conceptualizing a quality school. Such abstraction is necessary and valuable, but you also need to make this journey concrete and personal.

## TAKING A LOOK IN THE MIRROR

If you want to inspire quality in your school, you must put aside the seductive notion of talking about the "school," (an externalization and failure to accept responsibility) and look in the mirror. You have to figure out exactly what *you* expect to do and to get from being an educator. On an even more fundamental level, it would be helpful for you to figure out just how you go about satisfying your basic psychological needs.

*The Role Of Work*  How does work, specifically the world of education, fit into your quality world? What needs do you satisfy at work and how do you satisfy them? While many of us are drawn to the field of education for similar reasons, we bring our uniqueness as well.

■ **RELATIONSHIPS** Do you have important personal relationships at work? Is it a place where you are able to satisfy your need for belonging, at least to some degree?

■ **MORE THAN MONEY** Most of us work for more than money. Work is commonly valued, in part because it helps us meet our need for personal power and competence. Is that the case for you?

■ **MAKING A CONTRIBUTION** Do you perceive yourself as a competent professional, one who makes a meaningful contribution to the field of education? A meaningful contribution does not mean that you must be nominated as "Teacher of the Year." It may be your honest belief that the field has been enriched because of your efforts, that you have positively touched some lives.

■ **THE NEED FOR FREEDOM** What about the need for freedom? By its very nature, our commitment to work in a profession that runs according to a fixed schedule means we knowingly sacrifice freedom to a degree. Still, some educators feel a tremendous sense of freedom and others feel imprisoned. Honestly, what is it like for you?

■ **HAVING FUN** Finally, there is the need for fun. As I often say in my workshops, fun does not mean uninterrupted bliss. Anyone who has been in the profession for any length of time knows that there will be bad days and bad weeks. Some of us have even had our share of bad years. Still, when you look at things *over the long haul,* is work a place where you have fun? Is there a sense of joy in what you do? Do you still laugh with the students? With your colleagues? Is the laughter the ugly laughter that is steeped in cynicism, anger, and sarcasm, or the wonderfully pure laughter that signals an appreciation of the joy of living and learning together?

As you answer these questions, you will get an increasingly clear sense of how work fits into your quality world. Here's another way to ask yourself some of the same questions:

If you were to lose your job tomorrow, what would you lose other than money and any security that you believe you have? How you answer that question will help you identify just what work means to you.

I urge you to take a long time and reflect upon these questions seriously. If you find the questions uncomfortable or irrelevant, try to determine where those thoughts are coming from. In my experience, there are a great many people who are wonderfully skilled at discussing issues provided they are able to adopt a safe, detached position. Some of these people are well-versed in choice theory. But choice theory is useless if it is nothing more than a theoretical framework. Its value is only realized when it is given life by being put to use. Put simply, it is not enough to "talk the talk." We also need to "walk the walk."

We can't talk about "universal basic psychological needs" and ignore that we have these needs. The quality world is not simply a theoretical abstraction I use to describe and categorize *others;* it applies to *me* as well. Considering how working in the field of education adds quality to your life is far from irrelevant. It may be one of the most relevant things you do. If you find the questions uncomfortable, invite the discomfort into your consciousness and discover what it can teach you. You may learn something valuable. You may find new ways to make work more meaningful and enrich your daily experiences.

When I do this kind of activity with groups of teachers, there are usually a number of participants in the workshop who discover that teaching adds quality to their lives in ways they hadn't realized. They begin the activity with an amorphous sense that they enjoy their jobs (even with all the frustrations) but they are at a loss to say exactly *why* teaching is so satisfying to them. By seriously reflecting upon their own quality words, their own needs, and their own behavioral choices, they come to appreciate why teaching is so important to them. The experience for these teachers is affirming, but it is more than that. It is a clarification. These teachers discover that their most important values in life and their behaviors as teachers are congruent. They discover that teaching is meaningful to them because it flows naturally from them, that their individuality is genuinely expressed as they responsibly carry out their roles as educators.

---

### Pete's Pathogram: An Activity

Here's an activity to help you clarify both the strength of your needs and the effectiveness of the behaviors you currently use to meet those needs. The activity, developed by Dr. Arlin Peterson of Texas Tech University, is entitled "Pete's Pathogram" used with his generous permission. Use the following chart to help you work your way through the pathogram.

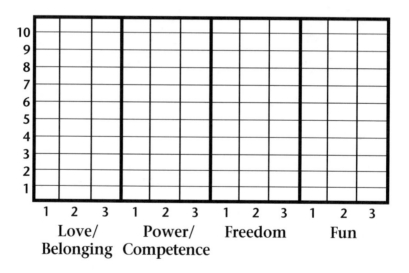

Because I am stressing the personal, the inside-out approach to building quality, I would ask you to complete two pathograms. The first will be personal and global, while the second will focus on school-related issues. Both should prove valuable, but provide you with very different kinds of information.

Let's begin with the personal, global pathogram.

**Column one:** Above each of the four universal basic psychological needs, answer the following: *How much time and energy do I currently spend behaving in ways that help me satisfy this need?* For example, consider the need for love and belonging. On a scale of 1 - 10, subjectively determine how much of your time is spent on behaviors that help you express your need to love and connect positively with others. If you believe you spend a lot of time behaving in ways that help you express your need to love and belong, give yourself a high rating. If, in your opinion, your behaviors do not lend themselves to expressing love and belonging, rate yourself lower. The rating is subjective, but consistent with the choice theory concept of self-evaluation. After having done this for love and belonging, similarly consider the needs for power, freedom, and fun. How much time and energy do you devote to behaviors that help you follow your genetic instructions to be powerful, to be free, and to be playful?

**Column Two:** Ask yourself the following question: *How much of this do I currently see myself having in life?* For example, do I see myself as loving and connected to others? Do I feel powerful, recognized, competent, listened to by others? How much freedom do I believe I have in my life? (Notice again, the importance of self-evaluation. On an "objective" level, two people may have equal amounts of freedom. Their perceptions, however, may be very different, and it is these subjective perceptions which will drive their behavioral systems regardless of "objective" reality.) Finally, how much fun do you think you have in your life? (Some years ago I worked with a woman who discovered through this process that she had been letting others define her for years. "You don't have enough fun," they told her, and she let their perception of fun and their perception of *her* control her. By doing this activity, she was able to self-evaluate and discover that she *really* did know how to have fun and was much more successful in this area than she had realized. Her new perception significantly altered her self-esteem in a positive way.) Again, self-evaluate and rate yourself in each need area from 1-10.

**Column Three:** Consider the following: *how much of this need you would like to have?* This area clarifies the fact that the strength of needs varies from person to person. Just as we receive different genetic instructions that tells us how tall to grow and determine our eye color, we also receive genetic instructions relative to the basic psychological needs. While the vast majority of us fall within an expected range, there is still some variation relative to how strong each need area is. For this section, ask yourself the following, focusing on outcomes: How much love and belonging do I want in my life? How much power? How much freedom? How much fun? Some of you may find it more helpful to focus on process instead of outcomes. If that's true for you, ask yourself the following: How much to I want to be a loving person, one who has strong connections to others? How strong is my need to be competent, to achieve, to master new skills? How important is it to me to behave in ways which express my need for freedom? How am I driven by a need to be playful and have fun? While each of the needs is important, you may discover that one or two of the needs are *more* important to you.

On the opposite page is an example of a completed pathogram and some comments on how to use the information it provides.

On a theoretical level, an *ideal* pathogram would be one which would have the three variables almost equally rated in any given need area. That does not mean that each need area would be equally strong, but that within any given need area, the three variables would share close to the same ranking. That would suggest that I put in a certain amount of time and energy, get back an amount consistent with my expenditure, and perceive that I am getting almost as much of that need as I want. The drive to have a little bit more than we currently have is natural, not patho-

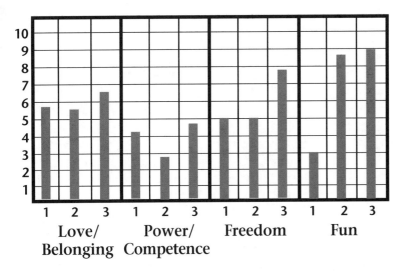

logical, and what keeps us striving to add quality to our lives regardless of how successful we are. (This ideal is illustrated in the sample love/belonging area.)

As the sample pathogram illustrates, however, things generally don't work out so smoothly in the real world. You are likely to find discrepancies within each need area.

What can these differences tell you? If you are putting in considerable time and energy (column 1), but that need area is not very well satisfied (column 2), it suggests that your behaviors are not as effective as they could be (illustrated in the power area). If this is the case, motivation is clearly not your problem. You want something and are willing to put in the time and energy to get it, but your efforts are not paying off as well as they might.

One possible solution: look at your current behaviors and determine which are more effective and which are less effective; then, create a better match between your effort and your return.

Suppose the first two columns are roughly equal? In that case, you would know that your efforts are reasonably effective.

If those two columns are lower than what you want (column 3), you have a whole different problem, illustrated in the freedom area of the sample pathogram.

Since your behaviors are reasonably effective, you most likely have to spend more time and energy in that area to get as much as you want.

From time to time, people discover that they have more than they want in a given area or more than their efforts would suggest they "deserve" (column 2 is higher than column 1 or column 3). If you have more than you want, look at how you can cut down on behaviors in that area. If you are getting more than expected, illustrated in the fun area of the sample, you might be thankful but also become more intentional about your behaviors in the future. Choice Theory does not deny the existence of good luck. Perhaps you have had some, but it may not last forever and it would be wise to be prepared for the time when your luck changes.

Don't be surprised if you find that you have a need area that is out of balance. It is not unusual for people to discover this. At first it may seem to be disconcerting news, but you can use this information to take more effective control of your life. The less effective person filters the information in a way which includes considerable emotion. For example, after discovering that I put a lot of time and energy seeking to meet my need to love and belong but have less of that in my life than I desire, I label the information as "sad" or "unfortunate." The more effective person, while not distorting the facts, is able to take in the information with less debilitating emotion attached to it. This information is seen as "interesting" instead of "unfortunate," and the person seeks to find ways to use it in a way that will help them get more quality in their lives.

The ability to see things less emotionally is a valuable skill for those wishing to gain more control over their lives. Choice theory helps us appreciate the value of seeing things as clearly as possible, not allowing our emotions to cloud our vision, and helps us remain focused upon the future so we can seek responsible solutions when we face challenges.

## School-Related Issues

After having completed the personal and global pathogram, I would suggest you complete one that relates to school. The process is the same but it is focused exclusively upon your professional life. Now you look at how much time and energy you expend in school-related behaviors that help you be loving, powerful, free, and playful. You then look at how much you believe you actually are loving, powerful, free, and playful, as it relates to school. Finally, you evaluate how much you want to be loving, powerful, free, and playful in your professional life. Again, you will gain some helpful information from this exercise, especially when you compare it to your more global pathogram.

Some of you may find that a particular need area asserts itself more in school than it does generally. You may discover that another need, very important to you in general, is not so important when you look exclusively at school. The information you get here can provide you some direction about how to make school more of a quality experience for you. By bringing your behaviors more into line with your wants, you will increase your level of satisfaction in most cases.

Pete's Pathogram has proven to be a helpful tool to many. It illustrates that the needs are not necessarily of equal strength. It helps us determine if our behaviors are effective. It points us in a direction when we discover things aren't working as well as we'd like.

## Additional Thoughts

Before we move on, here's some thoughts for those of you who are frustrated by all the theory and want to "cut to the chase."

■ **ACTION-ORIENTED** Reality therapy is action-oriented, but people can jump into action too quickly. There is a difference between behaving impulsively and taking decisive, effective action. If you know yourself to be someone who might have a tendency to move ahead "just to get things going," please slow down. It may help you to remember the concept of total behavior. By perceiving behavior as consisting of four components, you can free yourself from the notion of behavior exclusively as acting.

■ **THE THINKING FACTOR** While acting is one component of total behavior, so is thinking. The decisive person will utilize his thinking skills and make sure that there has been appropriate reflection before engaging in overt action.

■ **DOES IT FEEL RIGHT?** Attend, too, to the other components of total behavior. Does the course of action you are considering "feel" right to you? Reality therapy may be action-oriented, but we want to make sure our overt actions are congruent with our thoughts and feelings. Notice the physiological component as well. While this may be more subtle, try to get a "gut feeling," a bodily signal that helps you determine if a considered course of action is appropriate for you.

When you consider behavioral options from several perspectives, taking full advantage of the concept of total behavior, you will discover that your actions will be much more effective and decisive. You will have fewer instances of being "pulled in different directions." There will be fewer "approach-avoidance" experiences. Just as importantly, when you do get those uncomfortable feelings, you will respect them as important signals and check all of the components of your behavioral system before moving ahead.

There is considerable evidence that people who have a clear vision of what they want are more successful. That doesn't mean that knowing what you want in any way guarantees success. It does mean that you have a greater chance of achieving your goals when you are more certain of what you want.

There is also considerable research to suggest the positive impact of visualization. Those of us who can clearly visualize ourselves being successful in specific circumstances maximize our chances of making that happen. A number of successful professional athletes routinely use visualization techniques and enhance their performance.

■ **IMPORTANCE OF A MISSION STATEMENT**  How does this relate to you and to inspiring quality in your school? I would suggest to you that many of us enter this profession with very little notion of exactly what we want. We may value education. We may genuinely like children. We may believe in the importance of public education. But too few of us develop a personal mission statement about our professional role. (Mission statements are very much in vogue as I write this. I have seen them posted in hotel lobbies, businesses, and even fast food restaurants.) I think it's wise for each of us to develop our own personal mission statement.

A mission statement is a almost a personal Constitution. You may think of it as a map, a guide to help you as you make your way in the world. We all know people who we define as "solid," whose behavior seems consistent, purposeful, and not subject to momentary whims and transient feelings. We also know people whose behavior is much more arbitrary. These people seem externally controlled, subject to whatever immediate concerns present themselves, but lack that solid foundation and sense of purpose that most of us respect. The people in the first group have developed their own personal mission statement. They know who they are, what they value, what's really important to them. They have a system that allows them to evaluate their behaviors. Whether they know they have this "mission statement" in place is irrelevant. They do. The people in the second group don't have such a frame of reference. They may be as intelligent, as committed, as "good" as their counterparts, but they are trying to get somewhere without a map—without a clear sense of where they want to go.

Which type of person would you rather be? Which type of educator would you rather be? Do you have a personal mission statement? A professional mission statement? (Not one written for your school or district, but one composed by you and for you outlining your mission as an educator.)

How do you know if you have a mission statement? Could you be one of those people who has one unconsciously? Let's find out.

First, let's just look at personal issues, not specifically professional ones.

- Would you say that your life is characterized by consistency in how you act?

- Are you more likely to act in very different ways in similar circumstances depending upon your mood or whatever outside factors happen to be present at any given moment?

- If you are a parent, pretend for a moment that you were your own child, would you be able to predict how you as a parent would act in a given situation with reasonable accuracy? What about if you were another family member?

If you can answer "Yes" to these questions without much difficulty, you probably have unconsciously developed a personal mission statement that has evolved over time and governs your behavior, at least in this domain. It is this central force in your life that allows you to behave with a level of consistency and fortitude even in difficult situations. It allows you to "do the right thing" even though another, easier path may present itself from time to time.

So let's assume you have evolved your own personal mission statement unconsciously. Do you want to write it down? Would it be worthwhile to really examine your core beliefs and values, to articulate what it is that governs your day-to-day behavior? If you believe that it would help you live an even more effective life if you were to write out your personal mission statement, do it now.

# DEVELOPING A PROFESSIONAL MISSION STATEMENT

Now let's turn our attention to the field of education. What is your mission as an educator? What do you *really* want to accomplish in your career? Without being grandiose or narcissistic, what contribution do you hope to make to this field? We *all* have something to contribute to our profession. What do you want your contribution to be?

## From Memories to Remedies

For some of us it is difficult to write a professional mission statement in isolation. It may be helpful to look into our past and re-familiarize ourselves with role models who help us clarify what we want to be as educators.

David Hardy, an instructor for The William Glasser Institute, has developed an activity he calls "From Memories to Remedies." Briefly, this activity allows us to remember some of the most important and valued teachers we had as students, to reflect upon what specific behaviors they used to help the classroom be the classroom an inviting place to grow and learn. As we recall these mentors and what exactly they did, we identify which of their positive behaviors we already have and which others we could add to our own repertoire.

I value what this activity can do for us as we create an image of who we want to be professionally, but I am also reminded of a quotation by Ralph Waldo Emerson: "The imitator dooms himself to hopeless mediocrity." Despite the sexism reflected in Emerson's comment, he gave us something of value: as we consult our own memories of educators who impressed us and added quality to our lives, we need to put our own stamp upon the images we create. How can you use what these people have given you in a way that reflects your individuality? Can you build upon their skills in a creative, unique way so that your students benefit from your individuality and uniqueness? "From Memories to Remedies" gives us a starting point. We need to tailor those memories to our own style and strengths and create something unique, something that reflects genuine quality.

If you have not done so already, I encourage you to begin writing your own professional mission statement. The process of developing this mission statement is at least as important as the product you end up with, if not more. This process allows you to seriously consider, perhaps for the first time, exactly what *you* want from the field of education. If you already work in the field, someone interviewed you as part of the application process. Somebody else probably gave you a job description which outlining *what others expected of you*. A personal mission statement goes beyond that. It captures what *you expect of yourself.* Somebody *else* asked you some of these questions, but there's a good chance you never asked yourself these same questions and provided answers designed for your own use. If you were like many of us in an interview situation, you worked hard to provide the *right* answers to questions about your educational mission. Well, this is no interview. This is just you and your professional life. So just between you and anyone else you choose to tell, what exactly do you want from this profession?

If you have not yet entered this most noble profession, please carefully consider this issue before going any further. While I have great respect for the majority of my colleagues there are some among us who really should not be in this field. Some people can live comfortably with this fact provided that there aren't "too many" teachers in this category. Try telling that to a student who has *that* teacher. Try telling that to the parent of a student who has *that* teacher. Try telling that to a teacher who has to work with *that* teacher. And finally, imagine what it must be like to *be* that teacher—to come to work day after day, year after year, unhappy, unfulfilled, uninspired. I honestly believe these people have much to offer, but not in their current situation. If only they had developed a professional mission statement they might have found the place where they can flourish and grow into satisfied, fulfilled, and enlivened people.

Please do yourself a favor and develop your own professional mission statement. A few of you might find you will be more satisfied in another profession. Many more of you will become further committed to this field and more clear about what it is that you hope to do professionally-adding meaning and quality to your life.

---

### When Do I Begin?

Now. It's easy to read about mission statements and think to yourself, "That's really interesting. I should do that sometime." Or to delude yourself into thinking that you have a well-defined mission statement when you don't. What do you really want? Until you take the time to seriously consider, process, and *work* through this issue, you will not have a sufficiently clear vision and the solid foundation you need to move forward. Begin developing your mission statements, both personal and professional, right now. That doesn't mean you stop everything else, but begin the process now. Take time to think about these issues. Set aside time to write down your thoughts. Set some type of realistic timetable for yourself with the knowledge that your mission statements are always in a state of evolution. (If a mission statement is analogous to a personal Constitution, it may be helpful to remember that the Constitution is a living document, amended and interpreted differently, but providing a structure and framework that identifies us to ourselves and others). Don't let the evolving nature of mission statements be your excuse for not beginning your work now.

As you begin the process of developing your personal and professional mission statements, here are some questions to consider:

1. What values are most important to me, both personally and professionally?

2. Work is one way to give meaning and definition to my life. What do I think is important in the field of education?

3. How do I wish to be remembered, both personally and professionally?

4. I have opinions about many things. Which ones do I care about passionately?

After having drafted your mission statements, I hope you have enough information to more precisely answer the following question: "What do you want as an educator?" With your mission statement to guide you, you should be able to articulate a quality world vision of what it means to you to be part of this profession. If you have completed the activities offered to you in this chapter, you have a better understanding of your basic needs and know which ones may be more important to you.

### Vision Of A Quality School: An Activity

It is time to synthesize this information and create an individual vision of a quality school. Keeping in mind the notion of personal responsibility and control, try to focus on your own behavior in a quality school without thinking about others, regardless of how vital a role they may play in the overall functioning in the school. Later on, we will examine a way in which to forge a collective vision. At this point, however, the focus needs to remain on you.

- What is your vision of a quality school? Specifically, what would you be doing in such a setting?

- Just as importantly, what kind of behaviors would we *never* see you engage in if you were to visualize yourself in a quality school?

- What kinds of things would we hear you say in a quality school? To students? To administrators? To colleagues? To parents?

- What kind of things would you *never* say in a quality school? To students? To administrators? To colleagues? To parents?

Answer these questions individually and then discuss them with others in your school who are interested in these ideas. It's not important that they be well-versed in choice theory or reality therapy. They need only be interested in finding ways to make schools better and be willing to look at and discuss their own behaviors as they consider improving our schools. The comments offered by your colleagues are only there to help you more clearly define your vision of a quality school.

At the conclusion of this individual activity and any discussions you may have with colleagues, you should be able to clearly articulate your vision of a quality school. As much as you will be tempted to talk about what the *school* will be like and what the *students* in such a school will be like, focus on what *you* will do and say in such a setting. This is all part of inspiring quality from the inside out.

Before moving ahead, I encourage you to write out your personal vision of a quality school. If it is helpful, remember that this vision is always evolving. As you gain new insights and new information and as you begin to discuss these ideas with others, your ideas may change. At each point, however, your vision represents your best current understanding of a quality school and your behavior within that vision.

Before you begin the next chapter, consider where you are on this journey toward inspiring quality in your school. If you have begun to do the activities suggested in this chapter, you are now moving from theory to practice. You have begun to more clearly identify yourself and your role within a quality school using choice theory concepts, basing your actions upon a solid theoretical foundation.

# CHAPTER 6

# *What Are You Doing?*
# *& Self-Evaluation*

## WHAT ARE YOU DOING?

In the previous chapter, you developed a vision of who you want to be as an educator. That vision is critical because it serves as a frame of reference or standard against which you can measure your performance. Simply having a vision or mission statement is not enough. The next phase in the journey is to examine your current behavior. Give serious thought to the following questions:

- What exactly do you do as an educator?

- How do you behave on a day-to-day basis?

- How do you behave in a crisis?

- How do you structure your classroom?

- How would you describe your teaching style?

- How do you assess student performance?

- How do you manage unwanted behavior?

- How do you interact with your teaching colleagues? With the administrators? With the support personnel?

- How do you perceive parents? The school board? The central office administrators?

Superficial, cursory answers to any of these questions will not inspire quality in your school. Honest examination of what you *do* will move you toward quality.

The most productive way to look at these issues is to examine your day. Then determine if your current behaviors are consistent with the mission statement you developed earlier. Your mission statement embodies your most important values. It is not unusual, however, for people to behave in ways that are at odds with their own values or mission statement. If you find this is true for you, be assured that you are not alone. Many of us *really do* believe what we say we believe, yet still behave in ways which contradict our own values.

How can you avoid that pitfall? The first step is awareness. Many of us who act in ways inconsistent with our values are unaware of it. It's not until it is pointed out to us that we even realize that we have a problem. By seriously processing the questions posed in this chapter, you can get a clearer sense about how congruent your behavior is with your values.

## "THIS IS JUST AWFUL" VERSUS "HOW CAN I USE THIS INFORMATION?"

To a very large extent, we create our own reality. To illustrate, let's consider the case of a student not unlike a student you may have encountered at some point in your career. This particular student is doing quite poorly in your class and is in danger of failing for the year. You are confident that with reasonable effort, the student has a legitimate chance to pass despite how poorly he is currently doing. You tell the student about his current situation and his future prospects. At this point, the student literally creates his own reality about this particular situation. This reality will go a long way in determining his course of action and, in turn, will play a major role in whether he passes or fails.

What options are available to the student once you make him aware of his status? Theoretically, the options are infinite and based upon his personality, your presentation of the information, your relationship with the student, the family background, etc. Still, most options fall into two large camps:

1. "This is just awful."

This emotionally charged way of coding the information generally leads to behaviors that are panic-driven and less effective.

2. "How can I use this information?"

In this scenario, information is received and processed rationally, not emotionally. While things don't always work out the way we want, we have a better chance of being successful when we put ourselves in a position where we can access and use any information available.

Back to our hypothetical student for a moment. If he uses the "this is just awful" lens to perceive the situation, he will likely remain unsuccessful. How he plays out his failure will depend upon a number of factors. He may choose to be paralyzed by the information. He may use the bad news as an excuse to give up. He may defend himself with anger or adopt an "I don't care" attitude. Regardless, he will continue to fail because he has perceived the information you provided in a way that will perpetuate his failure.

On the other hand, what will happen if he creates his reality from a "how can I use this information?" point of view? Since he now has made the choice to make this information available to him in a helpful way, he can utilize it to his advantage. He is more apt to choose an effective way to deal with the information. He is more likely to figure out what needs to be done in order to pass, assuming this is something he wants. He is able to make better decisions because he is more rationally driven and his judgment and perceptions are less distorted by his emotions (valuing filter).

Consider this situation with the concept of total behavior in mind. The "this is just awful" behavior is *feeling* dominant, whereas the "how can I use this information?" approach is fueled by the *thinking* component of total behavior. As was discussed, it is generally easier to remain in more effective control of our lives when our total behavior is led by our thoughts and actions rather than our feelings and physiology.

Interestingly, in both of the situations presented about our hypothetical student the "real world" is the same. Reality is no different. What is different is how the student chooses to perceive reality. That, in turn, impacts his future behaviors.

Looking at a situation about a student can be easier than looking at our own situation. At this point, I'd invite you to look at the information you received when you answered the questions posed at the beginning of this chapter. Are you willing to look at it from the "how can I use this information?" perspective even if your immediate tendency is to adopt the "this is just awful" position? How does this perceptual shift change things? Will your behavior be different because you see things differently? If so, how will it be different? Do you believe that you can decide how to see things without denying the truth? (This is a major issue and will tell you a lot about the kind of person you are. Essentially, you are being asked to decide if you believe you are controlled by external events or if you actively determine what outside events mean and how you will act upon that information.) Does it help you to see things from a particular point of view? What, if anything, prevents you from doing this?

# KEEPING A JOURNAL/LOG

Answering the question "What are you doing?" is simultaneously easy and difficult. The difficult aspect for many of us is simply trying to remember all of the things we actually *do* during the course of a day, a week, or even a class period. One way to help you is to begin keeping a log or journal in which you write

## Sample Journal/Log Page

**Mission Statement:** (The "What I Want" from my job statement. This remains constant, even though circumstances change.)

**Time Frame:** (ie. Tuesday, May 4; Period 7; 9:30 - 10:30; etc.)

**What I did:** _____

_____

_____

_____

down as much as you can remember about what you do in a given time period. Here's one suggestion about how to organize and utilize such a log. The format is essentially unimportant as long as you get the information you need to help you make the gains you want to make.

The value of keeping a log is that it gives you the chance to practice tracking your own behavior. Sometimes it's easy to be so involved in what we're doing, that we are literally unaware of what we do. Is it any wonder that some of our behavior runs contrary to our stated values and mission? The log gets you back in touch with the many behaviors that have become so habitual that you unintentionally engage in them. By becoming more consciously aware of what we do, we can measure our actions against our central values and mission. Over time, we can become more conscious of our everyday, routine behavior and bring a greater degree of intentionality into our lives. This is something I value very much. I want what I do to be done with intention, not because I was unaware of the impact and meaning of my behavior. Anything I can do, personally or professionally, which increases my level of intentionality furthers my growth and development and allows me to become more of the person I want to become.

## SELF-EVALUATION

Self-evaluation is the key component of the reality therapy process. At this point you have developed both a quality world picture (helped by the creation of a mission statement) and identified your current behaviors (using a log of your behavior or something similar). Now is the time to hold up the mirror and ask yourself how satisfied you are with your current level of success. This may be the most difficult part of your journey, but it is the part that will result in your greatest gains if you are willing to encounter this part of the process with total honesty and courage.

What gives us the courage to engage in honest self-evaluation? It is the belief that this process will help us discover ways to maintain those things in our lives which represent quality and to improve those areas which fall short of the mark. The purpose of self-evaluation is continuous improvement and growth. It is not undertaken so that we will feel bad, or guilty, or less than successful. None of those feelings and the total behaviors that accompany them will help us add quality to our lives. We engage in self-evaluation in because we want to:

- take stock of where we are,

- affirm what we are doing well,

- get an clear sense of how we can become more successful.

It is rare for anyone, regardless of their level of success and competence, to engage in honest self-evaluation and *not* identify areas in which they could improve. If I can say with total honesty that I am a very good parent, that does not mean that I cannot become an even better parent. So self-evaluation almost always leads to some acknowledgment that we could do more. Many of us already feel stretched as it is. We feel as if we are pulled in too many directions and have enough things competing for our limited time and energy. Engaging in honest self-evaluation may add even more to what we believe we *need* to do. It is no wonder why many of us avoid self-evaluation. It means more work.

---

### Why Get Involved?

With that in mind, why would anyone wish to become involved in the process of self-evaluation? Well, on one level we self-evaluate whether we realize it or not, whether we *want to* or not. We automatically evaluate the effectiveness of our behaviors and continue or modify our behaviors based upon the feedback we receive from the outside world. This nonconscious form of self-evaluation occurs regardless of whether we have heard of choice theory or not—whether we believe the theory or not.

The self-evaluation I am referring to in this discussion is different in that it is both conscious and intentional. I consciously decide that I want to evaluate how successful I am in a given situation and I do that by referring back to my quality world picture or mission statement. By making this conscious decision to evaluate my behaviors against the quality world picture I have developed, I increase the chances of living a congruent life. People who live congruently have aligned their quality world visions and daily behaviors. What they do at any given moment seems to flow naturally. While they may sometimes experience difficult interactions with others, they seem less internally conflicted than many of their colleagues. Such people are often described as "centered" or "grounded." If those are words that you would like used by others when they think of you, you may want to practice intentional self-evaluation.

An added benefit of conscious, intentional self-evaluation is that it can help you manage stress and prioritize your values. Many of us feel overwhelmed by the many things we believe we need to do. Self-evaluation with reference to your personal mission statement can help you more clearly see what things *really* are most important to you. We have all heard stories of people who discovered their true values and established their priorities when confronted by a horrible tragedy or crisis. You don't need to experience disaster to develop such clarity of purpose. Intentional self-evaluation can provide the same clarity so you can more easily sort through things and quickly determine which things really deserve your energy and attention and which are less important, even trivial.

### Finding The Time To Self-evaluate

People sometimes wonder how they will find the time to intentionally self-evaluate, when they already feel too busy as it is.

Stephen Covey provides a valuable activity and way of conceptualizing how we live our lives in his book *The Seven Habits of Highly Effective People*. Essentially, Covey divides activities into four areas or quadrants: I. Important-Urgent; II. Important-Not Urgent; III. Not Important-Urgent; and IV. Not Important-Not Urgent. Virtually every activity in which we engage can be put into one of these four areas.

Examples Covey gives are:

Quadrant I. Crises and Pressing Problems;

Quadrant II. Planning, Recreation, Relationship building;

Quadrant III. Interruptions, Popular activities, Some calls;

Quadrant IV. Trivia, Busy work, Time-wasters (p. 151).

Every one of us, including those who claim to have "no time," spend some time on activities that can be identified as "Not Important - Not Urgent" (Quadrant IV). These are activities which we can abandon without compromising the quality of our lives. This will give us additional time to spend on those activities we have ignored because we have identified them as "important, but not urgent." Inspiring quality in your school may fall into this category. Everyone would agree it is an important notion but we tell ourselves that it is something we can address sometime in the future, further deluding ourselves with the fantasy that it will be addressed in the "near" future.

We self-evaluate because we are driven to continuously improve our lives. I urge you to adopt a global perspective when we consider the concepts of self-evaluation and continuous improvement. There is a danger in taking too narrow a view that can lead to what I think is pathological self-evaluation.

Let me offer an example to illustrate this point. Several years ago, it was time to paint the trim on my house. Before applying a new coat of paint, the existing paint had to be scraped and primed. Any of you who have scraped paint and sanded know that it is almost always possible to improve what you have done. Taken to extremes, the job can literally last forever. As I scraped and sanded, I evaluated how well I had done and compared that to an idealized quality job of scraping and sanding.

At some point I made the decision that what I had accomplished was legitimately "good enough," knowing full well that I could have continued working and improved my performance. By taking a wider view, however, I was able to ask myself the following questions: What will I gain by continuing to improve the quality of *this* job? How will my life be better? What are the costs associated with continuing? Considering the kind of person I want to be (mission statement), is it better for me to continue working or to stop at this point? In all honesty, I could answer that the quality of the work I had done would not be appreciably improved with additional effort. But the time I could have conceivably spent in the name of continuous improvement was significant. It might have prevented me from having time to play with my children, to take a bike ride, to go out to dinner with my wife. Each of those activities adds quality to my life. By intentionally self-evaluating with a generalized mission statement and vision of the person I want to be, I could "see the big picture" and not get "bogged down in the details."

Use this more global notion of a quality life when practicing intentional self-evaluation. As a former English teacher, I know very well that there is no piece of writing which cannot be improved. I want my daughter who recently began her college education to be a competent writer. When she produces an essay English class, I want her to do it with the concept of quality in mind. However, I don't want her to spend so much time on her English essay that she ignores her other school responsibilities. And I don't want her to spend so much time on school work that she does not leave time to fully immerse herself in campus life and do the other things essential to growing up and developing her identify as an independent young adult.

By keeping our eye on "the big picture," we will prevent ourselves from losing our way and getting caught up in the minutia. The pursuit of quality, unchecked, can lead to a life that is painfully out of balance. Truly healthy people find ways to live balanced lives so that they can follow all of their genetic instructions as they pursue quality in everything they do. Easy to write. Hard to do.

# SELF-EVALUATION: AN ACTIVITY

Go back to the log introduced earlier in this chapter. With the concept of self-evaluation in mind, add the following component to your log:

## Sample Journal/Log Page

**Mission Statement:** (The "What I Want" from my job statement. This remains constant, even though circumstances change.)_____

_____

**Time Frame:** (ie. Tuesday, May 4; Period 7; 9:30 -10:30; etc.) _____

**What I did:** _____

_____

_____

_____

**Self-Evaluation:** Is this behavior consistent with my Mission & Values (ie. In the long run, does it help me become more like the educator I want to be?)_____

_____

_____

_____

# CONCLUSION

The purpose of this chapter has been twofold:

- To help you examine your current behaviors, especially as they relate to your mission statement.

- To help you self-evaluate and determine how successful your current behaviors are when you consider your pictures, values, and mission.

The questions presented are easy to write and can be too easily read without giving them the thought they deserve. If you are serious about moving in a direction of increased quality, you will need to spend considerable time and energy examining your current behavior and measuring them against your own standards. This is a process of self-examination which takes time and effort. It is unlikely that you will discover that your behavior is always congruent with your mission. The tendency may be to adopt the "this is just awful" viewpoint, but you will be better off if you can utilize the "how can I use this information?" approach.

I wish I could provide more information about how to do this process of self-assessment and self-discovery, but the fact is each of you must find the way that works best for you.

What I can say based upon personal experience and stories from many colleagues is this: If you give these questions your time and energy and accept the information you receive, you will find ways to become personally and professionally more effective. It is unlikely if you do this that you will find it to be anything less than worthwhile, even if it requires a lot of hard work. It demonstrates that hard work is worthwhile when we discover that it adds quality to our lives.

# CHAPTER 7

# *Creating a Personal Action Plan*

Dr. Robert Wubbolding, senior faculty member of The William Glasser Institute, has developed a mnemonic device to help remember the core elements in the reality therapy process. Remembering the call letters of the fictional radio station WDEP can remind us that reality therapy helps people:

W–Identify what they want, the quality world picture that they have developed.

D–Determine what they are currently doing to achieve their wants, their present behavior.

E–Evaluate the effectiveness of their current behaviors.

P–Plan to continue those behaviors which they judge to be effective and plan more effective behaviors in those areas where they are less satisfied.

At this point, you have created a *quality world picture* (W), *determined* your current behaviors (D), and *evaluated* their success (E). It is now time to *plan* in order to add more quality to your life (P).

# MAINTAINING SUCCESS

As you evaluated your current behaviors, you no doubt discovered areas in which you are being very successful. For each of us, there are *some* areas where things are going well and our efforts are bearing fruit. It is easy to minimize our successes and move right into the process of improving where we have discovered shortcomings, but it is important to slow down. First acknowledge your successes and give yourself credit for those things you are doing well. It's important to build a strong self-concept and see yourself as someone who can be successful. You will need all of your strength and resources as this journey progresses so take time now to fortify yourself by acknowledging your success.

Your current successes, be they big or small, many or few, represent the foundation upon which you will build. That foundation must be strong and must be maintained if it is to support you on the way. I would not recommend that your first plans deal in any way with changing less effective behaviors. Instead I encourage you to reflect upon your successes and begin by developing plans to maintain whatever success you are currently experiencing. If you ignore this part of the process, you may find yourself in a continual cycle of frustration as you experience success after success and still feel empty, unfulfilled, and as if you are "getting nowhere." In that situation, your unmaintained and undernourished foundation erodes. New foundations are continually built and ignored. They, too, fall into disrepair and crumble. The result is the empty feeling that comes from successes built without the necessary structure to maintain them.

To avoid this too common cycle of frustration, make a firm commitment to plan behaviors designed to maintain your current successes.

- What, specifically, do you do that adds quality to your life, personally and/or professionally?

- What things are you doing that work well?

• How can you make sure that you don't unintentionally give up these effective behaviors that have helped you get this far?

People who are in good physical condition will quickly get out of shape if they give up the behaviors that have helped them get in shape. Teachers whose classes are in "good shape" will also be in serious trouble if they ignore those behaviors that have resulted in their current success.

Again, I am emphasizing the concept of intentionality. Sometimes we get lucky and develop successful behaviors non-consciously. One difference between those who remain successful and those who don't is that the successful people examine their lives, discover what works, and make sure to intentionally continue those behaviors that are effective.

For example, through the process of examining your current behaviors, you may discover that you routinely acknowledge students for their efforts and regularly treat them with dignity and respect. As you evaluate your classes, you may discover that you have fewer discipline problems than many of your colleagues even though you have students who are equally challenging. Over time, without a lot of conscious self-evaluation, you developed the behaviors of treating students with dignity and respect even when they behave in irresponsible and offensive ways.

By identifying what you did non-consciously, you can make this behavior more intentional. Make a plan to guarantee that you will always treat students with dignity and respect for two reasons. First, it is consistent with your personal mission statement and is an example of behaving in a way which is congruent with your vision of the professional you want to be. Second, through the process of self-evaluation you have discovered that this congruent behavior is an effective behavior, one which helps you inspire the kind of quality classroom you wish to have. There may have been some luck in developing these successful behaviors. There is, however, no luck involved when you intentionally decide to maintain patterns of successful behavior. This is an example of taking more effective control of your life.

## Making Discussions Effective

Regardless of your position in the school, you can have conversations with your colleagues. You can get together and talk about professionally important ideas. You can talk with your administrators and try to get their support.

The nature of those dialogues is critically important. If you present yourself as the "expert," the one person in the complex world of education who knows all the answers, others will avoid you. You will likely be more successful if you simply invite others to take part in an adventure, a journey designed to figure out how to make your school better. It makes no difference if your school is currently identified as "good" or "bad" or somewhere in the middle. The purpose of the journey toward quality is continuous improvement. There is no need to label, only to improve.

Discussions aimed at improving quality can easily erode into complaint sessions. Such sessions generally do little to inspire quality education. In fact, they almost always cause harm because those who participate leave the discussions feeling frustrated, demoralized, and drained of energy. If only a small group of teachers attend such discussion groups, it can set up an "us vs them" situation within the school, another enemy of quality. Discussions, therefore, need to be forward-looking and solution-oriented. Backbiting, blaming, scapegoating, and externalizing will not lead you toward quality. One way to measure the success of your conversations is to determine if people want to continue the dialogue. Conversations that are only thinly disguised gripe sessions quickly become a bore. Most teachers have enough meaningful things to do in their lives. They do not need to fill their lives and already busy schedules with conversations that are divisive and lead nowhere. Adopting the position that "we are here to fix the problem, not fix blame" is one way to minimize the chance of falling into the negativity trap.

If the administrators are not familiar with choice theory, reality therapy, and quality school concepts, they may be skeptical when you approach them. How you perceive their skepticism says at least as much about you as it does about them. Do you identify their reluctance as an unwillingness to look at new ideas? Do you see it as evidence of their conservative position and a failure to adopt new ideas and be on the cutting edge?

Perhaps you are right, but there may be another way to perceive their skepticism. Maybe they are skeptical because they have been in this profession for a long time and have heard and seen too many educational movements that have been short-lived and of little value. Maybe they know something about the staff and community that suggests to them that new ideas have to be introduced slowly and carefully. Maybe they need more information, that they have found they are more successful in the long run when they gather sufficient information before moving ahead. You can legitimately adopt either perception, so here's an evaluation question for you:

> If you want to inspire quality in your school, does it help you to perceive the administrators (or your other colleagues, or the parents, or the school board, etc.) the way you do? Is there another way to perceive them which is just as valid and would be more helpful to you, considering your goal to inspire quality in your school?

Building a quality school will likely be the most difficult professional work you have ever done. The real work involves learning how to interact more successfully with a large number of people. Most of us develop our own circle of acquaintances within our school community. We tend to associate with others who espouse similar values and beliefs. We naturally spend less time with those who are different from us. While this reflects "common sense," common sense alone will not help you inspire quality in your school. In a quality school, individuals intentionally work to develop better relationships with all of their colleagues, not just those to whom they are naturally drawn. What allows this to happen (not without difficulty, by the way) is a shared vision of what makes a quality school and how people behave in a quality school. Aligning yourself to this higher value allows you to reach out to others when you might otherwise find it easier to remain in your own "comfort zone."

Does it help you to see administrative skepticism in a negative way? What does that do to your working relationship? To your level of energy? To your level of commitment? To your ability to work effectively to inspire quality in your school? Would you be better served by seeing things differently? If you were able to see things in a more favorable light, what would happen? Would things be better? Worse? The same? Don't just read these questions think about them—answer them, discuss them with your colleagues. Let your future actions flow from the honest answers you generate.

If you decide that you would be better off seeing things differently, I have other questions for you. What prevents you from doing just that? Are you caught in the illusion that "I can't help it. That's just the way I am"? Are you so naive as to really believe that the way you see things now is "objective" and any other vision is less valid? These are important questions that need answers before you continue your journey. I implore you to take time and reflect upon these notions before moving forward. How you finally answer these questions will define how you see the world. Your world vision will impact every decision you make, both as it relates to quality schools and in a larger context.

---

*Other Things To Consider Doing*

■ **READING** It is important to educate yourself if you want to help facilitate significant reform within your classroom, school, or district. A number of schools are involved actively in discussing, defining, and implementing the quality school principles proposed by Dr. Glasser in *The Quality School.* They share a common belief in the principles of choice theory and utilize the process of reality therapy to help them move forward. If you haven't yet familiarized yourself with books detailing choice theory and reality therapy, as well as those that specifically address quality school issues, it will be worthwhile to take the time to read what has been written in this area. The "Suggested Readings" at the end of this book provide you with a list of recommended titles in the field.

■ **CONFERENCES/IN-SERVICE TRAINING WORKSHOPS** Other options to consider: attending presentations, workshops, or courses about choice theory and quality schools. As more and more schools become interested in these ideas, more opportunities present themselves to attend sessions that help you learn more about these concepts.

■ **INVOLVING STUDENTS** Talk with your students about quality and quality schools. One of the main principles in the quality school movement is to focus on and discuss quality. If we want to inspire quality work and improve the quality of our schools, we need to become intentional about how we address the issue.

Many of us have never discussed seriously quality and quality work with our students. We have taken the responsibility of determining what quality is and then assigned tasks designed to help students attain a level of proficiency we define as quality. Those dwindling number of students who have school and doing high level work in their quality worlds, succeed in school. Unfortunately, increasing numbers of students, for whatever reasons, do not achieve at the level we want. In order to change their current school behaviors we need to change their perceptions. One effective way to do that is to give them new information and engage them in discussions about quality.

---

***Approach With Caution*** Discussions about quality need to be approached cautiously. If you are the type of teacher who has done little or none of this in the past, you will be wise to proceed slowly. Don't begin by asking the students to discuss quality work and quality schools. There is a good chance many of them will find the topics irrelevant. Some may even be suspicious that you are trying to con them into doing better work. Instead, have the students identify topics of interest to them and have several brief conversations about quality relating to these topics.

Teachers frequently complain there is not enough time to have discussions about "trivial" topics; but, learning how to communicate orally, to defend a position, to respect the views of others, and to articulate your views clearly are fundamental academic skills I want my children to learn. The topic is of less importance to me than the skills being mastered. Encouraging students to choose topics to discuss and using their interests to explore the issue of quality seems to me to be time well spent. Keep in mind, too, that I am suggesting brief discussions. In nearly every class, including secondary school classrooms that are frequently burdened by too-short class periods and governed by a rigid bell schedule, ten minutes once a week can be found to engage in valuable discussion.

After several general discussions about quality, spanning several weeks to two months, the students will have enough evidence to convince them that you really do care about what they think and value their ideas. By itself, this will make your class more need-satisfying, and you may find the students more productive. At this point you can introduce the second phase of your discussions about quality. Now you can focus on the world of school.

Say something like this to the students:

> We've had a number of talks about quality. Let's talk about school for a while. If this classroom were an ideal classroom, what would it be like? What kinds of things would you see me do and hear me say? How would I behave? What kinds of things would I hear you say and see you do? How would you behave? As we have our discussion, let's remember what our jobs are in school.

This will lead to a lively discussion about what you currently do that represents quality and reveal areas where you can agree to grow together. Assuming you have enough involvement with the students, it is both appropriate and respectful to challenge them when they present their ideas. "How would that add quality to our classroom?" is a helpful question when asked sincerely, not sarcastically.

Discussions about quality classrooms should begin generally and gradually become more specific. Initially, you are trying to develop consensus about the environment and social behaviors in a quality classroom. When those generalities are sufficiently understood and agreed upon by everyone, including you, then you can move into discussions about specific units of study and assignments. With that foundation you can engage in a worthwhile discussion about what makes a quality essay, book report, term paper, home assignment, lab report, project, discussion, etc.

---

**Warning**

Over time, it may seem as if you have less "need" for discussions about quality. Beware of this trap. If you give up being intentional about quality, you will regress, slowly at first, but significantly. Before too long, you and the students may forget the importance of quality and fall back into old, less effective behaviors. Make sure you continue to talk about quality regularly. When you reach this maintenance phase, don't forget to continue to nourish what you have grown together over time.

---

# DEVELOP YOUR PERSONAL PLAN OF ACTION

It is time to develop your own personal plan of action. Your plan, like all plans, has the best chance of being successful when it incorporates the characteristics of an ideal plan. It should be specific, success-oriented, and something you can begin right away. The best plans will not be contingent upon the behaviors of others. Plan what you can do to inspire quality in your school *regardless of what others in the school choose to do.* This does not mean that your efforts won't be made easier if you have the support and energy of others. It does not mean that a school will not move faster and further with more staff involved. It does mean, however, that you are refusing to have your journey to quality contingent upon the behavior of others. You are proclaiming your right as an independent, active human being developing your own professional identity.

### Clarify Your Plan

If you think it would be helpful to write down your plan, do it. It doesn't really matter if you *like* the idea of putting a plan in writing. The key issue is for you to evaluate whether writing your plan will increase the chances of you becoming more like the person you want to be. If writing the plan down will not help you, of course it would be foolish to do so. Written or not, you need to have your plan clarified in order to begin. You need to know just what you will do, when, and how you will evaluate your progress. Without these specifics, you are likely to be less successful, to give up more easily, and to lose the opportunity to grow personally and professionally.

### Make A Commitment

After you have developed your plan, you need to determine just how committed you are to following through. For example, let's imagine that you included attending a choice theory, quality school workshop as part of your plan, are you *really* going to attend such a workshop, or are you only willing to "maybe" attend if one "happens" to be in the area "sometime soon"? While that might seem like a caricature, a great number of us are capable of developing tentative plans that "sound" great but lack the necessary commitment to make meaningful change. Just as the out-of-shape person needs to commit to a program of regular and meaningful exercise and a healthy diet in order to improve health and get in shape, you need to commit to a program that will involve real effort, time, and energy if you want meaningful improvement in your school. In short, everybody *wants* a quality school, the question becomes: How hard are you willing to work to develop one?

*Before moving to the next chapter: Have you developed your personal plan of action and are you committed to making it happen?*

# CHAPTER 8

# *Creating a Collective Vision*

In an earlier chapter, you were given an opportunity to create your personal vision of a quality school. It was suggested to you then that you keep your vision somewhat sketchy and not fully defined. If you were confused by that bit of advice, I hope you will soon begin to understand why I suggested the "cloudy" approach to envisioning a quality school.

Once you have everyone in a school, or at least a critical mass capable of effecting meaningful school-wide change, you are ready to begin the next phase of your journey. It is now time for everyone involved to come together and develop a shared vision of a quality school. Working together in a large group will require skills that perhaps you have not used regularly until now. To make things as easy as possible, remain focused on your objective and accept that what you are doing is hard work involving significant effort.

You want to leave this part of the process with a clearly articulated vision of a quality school that each person can embrace. It is not enough that everyone agrees that they can "live with" the group vision, for any vision to have energy and engage the staff, individuals must *embrace* the group's jointly-developed plan. Ideally, every person involved will feel as though their personal mission statement has been embodied by and incorporated into the school-wide mission statement. Rather than being a watered-down vision forged by compromise and concession, the ideal school-wide mission statement encompasses and transcends each individual contribution.

## DEALING WITH FRICTION

This will be an especially treacherous portion of your journey. Don't be surprised when you encounter trouble along the way. Friction is inevitable. The key will be how you deal with the inevitable problems you encounter. Now more than ever you will find that knowledge of choice theory and reality therapy can help you navigate in troubled waters.

### Working Together

Carefully attend to how your group functions. As you begin to work together, remember that the goal is to develop a group vision everyone embraces. Does your behavior indicate that you *really* mean that? Are you "walking the walk" or just "talking the talk"? Don't be surprised if you find that a small core of people dominate the group. Without quick and decisive action at this point, the group may falter before you know it. A number of people may feel left out, disenfranchised, and like they have been violated in some way. Ironically, those who dominate the group may be oblivious to the needs and feelings of the others. How is this possible?

### The Passionate People

Quite often, those who dominate in a group are passionate people with strong opinions. They get so caught up in the excitement of creating the vision that they are unaware of the group process. These people are often so focused on outcomes that they are oblivious to process. This is one of the things that makes inspiring quality in your school so difficult. There needs to be attention directed toward an outcome, a goal; there also needs to be a heightened sensitivity toward the process used to achieve the desired outcome. If the process is exclusionary or divisive, even unintentionally, the cost is too high. You may think you are on the road to quality when you articulate a vision that reflects the beliefs of a few powerful people in a system, but you are mistaken. Overtly or covertly, the alienated will behave in ways that will prevent you from ever getting to a place where there is high quality. You may have a wonderfully crafted mission statement, but you will lack your most important resource: the vitality and energy of everyone who is part of the system.

It is easy to read that last paragraph and come to the conclusion that the few passionate people who might dominate a group are "to blame." This is an illusion. Remember to use the reality therapy skills and choice theory knowledge you have. Will blaming anyone help you get more of what you want, in this case a quality school? Even if someone is "to blame," blaming will only make things worse. What is needed instead is a way to bring everyone together so that a true collective vision can be crafted, one which everyone can embrace. Blaming is at best a waste of time. Usually you will not be so lucky as to only waste time.

---

### Seeing All Sides

Just as there are generally several people in any group who tend to dominate, even unintentionally, usually at least one person in any group is more sensitive to group dynamics. This person is able to become excited by the passion of the more vocal but hears the silence of the less involved. The silence functions as a signal, alerting this person to the fact that something may be wrong, that the group may not be moving as smoothly as some believe. Using a knowledge of reality therapy and choice theory, this person can decide to take personal responsibility and get the group back together before things unravel.

Suppose this person is you but you feel somewhat uncomfortable about speaking up. It may be that you are being given an opportunity to grow, both personally and professionally. Maybe this is a chance to behave in a new, creative, and effective way. To see this as an opportunity to grow instead of an uncomfortable moment is using your ability to perceive things in a way that facilitates growth and leads to the creation of new, effective behaviors .

Another, more troublesome reality may explain your discomfort. Are you uncomfortable about speaking up for the good of the group because you feel as if you will somehow be hurt by those in power? If that is the case, your system is in serious trouble, especially if you are attempting to take a journey designed to inspire quality in your school. Somehow this issue needs to be addressed before the group moves on. When people believe they will be hurt by those in power if they do not act in a particular way, then the journey to quality is fraud.

This does not mean that those in authority never disagree or never behave in disagreeable ways. There will be arguments. People will continue to make mistakes in a quality school and behave in less than ideal ways in a quality school. Administrators will lose their tempers, teachers will lose their tempers, and students will lose their assignments. But the incidents will be few and the recovery will be swift. Most importantly, everyone will be free to express themselves honestly without fear of being hurt. When you feel as if you have something to say, but you are afraid that you may be "punished" in some way if you express yourself honestly, your system is coercive and pathological.

Exactly how do you behave if you find that there are people in the group who are feared? Again, I cannot give you *the* answer, for there is no *one* way to deal honestly and effectively with an issue this complex. I can, however, offer some guidelines and share some ideas. Most importantly, the behavior you choose must flow from who you are. It must be genuine or it will be of little value. Secondly, you need to make sure that *you* don't behave coercively or make fear your bedfellow when you try to resolve this dilemma. It may be tempting to *force* someone else into seeing things differently *for their own good.* Because of who I am, I would approach things directly. I would begin by making certain that my relationship with the person or people in question is solid. By this I mean that I want to make sure that they perceive me as someone who is there to help. If they believe that my actions are undertaken in an attempt to help, they will more likely trust me and be able to hear what I have to say. Without that trusting relationship there is little reason to believe that I will be heard. My efforts under those conditions will likely be counterproductive.

### A Matter of Trust

A trusting relationship is not something you can create upon demand. As a matter of fact, if you don't already have the trust required to engage in difficult conversations that may involve a degree of conflict and disagreement, there is almost no way to create it when you need it. The irony is that the trust is there precisely because you built it when it *wasn't* needed. You can be trusted because you have demonstrated over time that you are a person who genuinely wants to help people achieve quality. This is not to say that you are a person without an agenda. On the contrary, you are a person with a very specific agenda. But it becomes understood by all who know and work with you that your agenda, your goal, is to bring quality to everything you do. Seen in that light, others will trust and value you and you can provide the information that will help others behave in ways that will help the whole school move toward increased quality.

In almost every group there are a certain number of people who have strong views. Not surprisingly, these people frequently have leadership positions in the school. They almost always are people with a strong need for personal power. Because of the way most systems are set up, including most schools, these people may have not had the need to practice lead management. They are people with strong ideas and commitment to a cause. The power of their position linked with the power of their convictions has often been enough to help them get what they want. Many have additional skills, such as a charming personality or an ability to articulate their ideas in a clear and persuasive way. While those skills will continue to be valuable assets, they are not sufficient for those who wish to practice lead management.

---

### A New Type Of Manager

What is a lead manager and how does a lead manager differ from a traditional manager? Traditionally, managers have been viewed as "bosses," people who need to be obeyed because they hold power over us. This is not to say that bosses were not fair or humane. It simply emphasizes the point that everyone acted based on "the bottom line," the fact that bosses were to be obeyed or dire consequences could follow. Traditional boss managers used fear and coercion to get those working for them to do what they required.

Leaders have legitimate authority and accept the responsibility that comes with being in charge, but they operate very differently from traditional boss managers. Leaders understand that fear undermines quality work so the leader does everything possible to drive fear from the environment. Moreover, the leader realizes that no *one* person is as smart as the group. With that orientation, the leader actively seeks input and ideas from the workers. This does not mean that everything the workers suggest will be implemented. It does mean, however, that workers will be listened to and valued. Not surprisingly, workers who are lead managed find that their need for power is more satisfied. They are able to follow the genetic instruction to be powerful and to be recognized as someone with ideas worth considering. This, in turn, leads to increased in self-esteem which fuels increased production.

Quality schools, like all organizations, need to be managed. Effective lead management would be practiced by all managers in such a setting. Classroom teachers are managers of their classrooms. Lead management skills and behaviors can help classroom teachers create an environment where more students do more high quality work more often. While boss management may be successful in situations where compliance is the ultimate goal, lead management is necessary in settings where quality work is the objective.

A principal who is an effective lead manager is essential as you strive to develop a school-wide mission statement. This is the person who will help all of us discover where we want to take our school. This is the person who will make certain that each individual in the school feels valued and important. This is the person who will protect and appreciate our diversity, but help us forge a common vision so we can move forward together without compromising our individuality and creativity. A person with these important leadership skills is rare and schools with such principals are fortunate. Rare or not, this type of principal is what is needed to lead a school in its journey toward quality.

How is the collective vision formed, and what is the role of the lead manager/principal in this process? Everybody involved is encouraged to submit their personal mission statement in writing. If the number of staff members is small enough, everyone can get together to put together the school-wide vision. If numbers would make everyone's presence too cumbersome, then a representative group should be called together to draft a school-wide mission statement.

---

### Forming a Representative Group

Putting together a representative group requires skill, and if it is not handled well much of your effort will be wasted. I have heard about school systems that were very well-intentioned and didn't want to "burden" the staff with the "tedious" job of drafting a mission statement. Administrators put together their best guess of what would be a representative group. What is most important here is not so much *what* was done, but *how* it was done. In fact, the representative group might be *exactly* the same people the staff as a whole would have selected to represent them. However, because the staff was left out of the process of deciding who would make up the representative group, they felt alienated and disconnected to one of the most important things the school would ever do: develop a school-wide mission statement.

If a school is large enough to require a representative group to put together a draft, it is crucial that the staff select their representatives directly and that they trust them completely. Without that trust, the process will break down. I need to believe that what I have provided to my representative has been presented, listened to, respected, and valued. I need to know that my vision of a quality school is embodied in the whole. If I trust my representative and believe I have been part of creating this draft, even indirectly, I will support what is developed enthusiastically. Without that trust and belief that my contribution makes a difference, I will likely withdraw, behave with less enthusiasm, and my teaching may be characterized by indifference.

I have taken some time to talk about a representative group putting together a draft of a collective vision because it has been my experience that most school staffs are too big to directly involve everyone in this part of the process. Since it is not practical to directly involve everyone, it is imperative to effectively engage everyone, even indirectly.

## GATHERING FEEDBACK

Once a group has drafted a collective vision, it should be presented to the entire staff as just that: a draft for them to review and evaluate. I would suggest that copies of the draft be prepared for each staff member with a memo that says something like the following:

> The objective of our group has been to draft a vision that incorporates the thoughts of every staff member. Our efforts are now ready for your review. As you look at the draft we have developed, determine if what you gave to us individually has been captured in this collective vision. Perhaps some of the wording has been altered, but determine if your thoughts have been captured by this school-wide vision. This draft represents our best effort, but that does not mean that it cannot be improved. If you can offer any suggestions to strengthen our statement, we would be happy to consider your ideas. Thanks for giving this draft your serious thought and attention. We appreciate your feedback.

## REVISION AND ADOPTION

After receiving feedback, the representative group can revise the draft, as necessary. If significant changes have been made, it solicit additional feedback. If the changes that were made are minor, the group is ready to ask the staff as a whole to adopt the school-wide mission statement. When you ask the staff to adopt the statement, ask the following:

Will you support the following statement and behave in ways which are consistent with this statement? We have done our best to create a mission statement which honors our diversity and individuality, yet still identifies common principles in which we believe. We believe that our school will be even stronger if each of us commits to supporting this mission statement.

Consensus is reached when everyone agrees to publicly support the statement.

Creating a school-wide vision of a quality school is not trivial, superficial fluff. In doing this work, people are creating a meaningful foundation upon which to build their professional lives. Rather than reading in a book what they should do, they are engaging in the arduous process of self-reflection and self-evaluation. What they have developed will be the reference point upon which all future decisions in the school will be made. Rather than being lost at sea and rudderless, they are able to make decisions and move forward by evaluating whether their behavior is consistent with and supports their vision of a quality school.

Creating a school-wide vision of a quality school is more than just hard work, though. It is all that and more. It is a creative act of responsibility. It actively engages each staff member in the educational process. Done correctly, it has the power to energize and transform a school. It is exciting and fun. Good luck!

# CHAPTER 9

# *Creating a Collective Action Plan*

Once your school staff adopts a vision of a quality school embodying the diverse contributions of the entire group, you are ready to develop your collective plan of action. This is an exciting part of the journey. If you have arrived at this point having respected each other along the way, if you have reached this point without having people opt out, then you will now be energized by a glimpse of the light at the end of the tunnel.

What makes this part of the journey so exciting is the energy that is unleashed when a group has forged a vision which all support with enthusiasm. While it is perfectly understandable in cognitive terms and undoubtedly the fruit of hours of hard work and commitment, it feels especially exciting when you reach this point.

Anyone who has worked for years and felt isolated can appreciate the power and energy that greet you now. For too many years trainers skilled in reality therapy and choice theory provided workshops that were well received but had little impact over time. I can recall too many experiences when I provided this type of training. I facilitated what I thought was a quality workshop. The people who hired me were satisfied enough to recommend me to others, and the cycle went on. The only problem was that schools generally were not changed in any meaningful way. Some teachers were excited enough to try some new things in their classrooms, but there was not the total commitment on a building level required to make meaningful change. A few brave souls did the best they could, but most of them gave up after a while because they felt unsupported and isolated. It was not that their efforts were frowned upon by colleagues or administrators; they were discouraged because there was no all-encompassing vision and a plan of action. With a vision and plan, energy is released and significant positive change can be witnessed in a relatively brief period.

Developing a collective plan of action means that staff members develop a clear description of their roles. Everybody knows exactly who does what. Moreover, carefully scrutinized specifics ensure that roles and behaviors are congruent. In any large system it is easy to develop roles which will put people at cross-purposes. Anything that does that needs to be identified and explored so that internal consistency and constancy of purpose is maintained. The more internal inconsistency that remains, the more difficult it will be to inspire genuine quality.

When developing a collective plan of action, it is appropriate to look at the details. Until now I have suggested that you take a more generalized view of school function. Now it is time to get as specific and detail-oriented as possible. Those who have been frustrated by the more global discussion will now have their turn at the plate. Now that the groundwork has been carefully laid and the structurally sound foundation set, it is time to examine all the day-to-day, routine behaviors and events that make up a school. A host of issues need consideration at this point. The list varies from school to school, depending upon a host of variables. Still, a number of issues are fairly common and need reviewing by most schools embarking on this journey. In the following section, I have introduced seven common topics most schools need to consider as they decide how to develop *their* particular version of a quality school.

As you develop your collective plan, be sure that it has the following characteristics of a good plan.

## Success-Oriented

It should be success-oriented. Plans are constantly in a process of evolution so make sure that you develop plans that encourage success and keep you headed toward increased quality.

## Measurable

Plans should be measurable. How will you know if your school is better in two years? Five years? Ten years? What criteria will you set up so that you can reasonably evaluate your efforts? It is perfectly reasonable for community members to want *results* when you move in a different direction.

## More Than Nice

Quality schools should be places that are more than "nice" schools, "happy" schools, and "feel-good" schools. Serious education ought to be taking place and community members have the right to ask that you demonstrate results in some way. This illustrates the importance of community involvement and support as you explore quality school ideas. The more you undertake the process in an atmosphere of secrecy, the more the public will mistrust what you are doing. The mistrust will quite likely lead to a failure to provide support, including any financial support that might be necessary. If, however, you actively involve parents and other community members in the process of developing your school vision and plan, you can count on the support that will make your labor bear fruit.

## THE EVEN BIGGER COLLECTIVE VISION: AN ASIDE

The focus in this book has been on helping individual schools inspire quality using the concepts of choice theory and reality therapy. While I don't wish to digress too much, I want to remind you that most individual schools are only part of a larger system. As each school develops its vision, it should be looked at to determine if the entire system is internally consistent and complimentary. It is not so important that each school in a system be *exactly* alike. In fact, because they may serve students of different ages with different academic and social issues, some variations may be helpful. What is not productive, however, is having two schools in one district that have incompatible visions of what a quality school should reflect and what values are most important in the world of education. I have done some work for systems like that, where the component parts were very much at odds and there was no central, over-riding vision. The people working in those systems, regardless of their individual views had this in common: they were frustrated by the lack of a coordinated central vision and unhappy in their jobs.

# PART III

# *Inspiring Quality—Common Issues*

# CHAPTER 10

# *Topics to Discuss in A Quality School*

Everyone believes in quality. It is virtually impossible to find anyone—parent, teacher, or student—who would say that we shouldn't work to increase the quality of our schools. Any school trying to inspire quality will have to wrangle with these issues: homework, testing, grading, grade retention, ability grouping, co-teaching, and discipline/management. I provide my ideas on these issues on the following pages. You may find some of my opinions to be different from your collective vision; but taking the time to consider these issues so that your staff has a clearly defined notion of what constitutes a quality school for you is more important than agreement with me.

## HOMEWORK

This topic is one of the most explosive in American education. Many school districts have policies which articulate just how much homework should be given to students at various grade levels. It is difficult to find anyone, other than students, who will talk openly about the problem inherent in much of the homework assigned today.

At the risk of saying anything which you may find offensive, let me offer some potentially controversial thoughts about homework. These thoughts are provided only to give you something to consider and discuss with colleagues.

Some years ago, my older daughter was in junior high school and was given a homework assignment by her social studies teacher. Let me preface the story by saying that this particular teacher was creative, energetic, humorous, engaging, and helped the students truly appreciate the value of what he was teaching. My daughter enjoyed social studies more that year than any other, and I believe that she learned more in that class than she usually does in this area. With all that said, let me tell you a story about homework and the relationship it frequently has to quality academic work.

One evening I asked my daughter Kristy if she had completed her homework. She answered that she only had a social studies assignment to do and she had completed it. I asked her if I could see it. After looking at what she had produced, I asked her, "Kristy, does this represent your best work? Can you honestly tell me that you would evaluate this as quality?" She looked at me with a combination of bewilderment and anger. "Dad," she said. "I don't know what you're getting at. *It's only homework.*" When I asked her to explain that to me, she was glad to help me see things from her point of view. "You don't understand. This is just homework. If I do it, I get a check mark. If I don't do it, I get a zero. I'll get a check for this. This is good enough. I'll get a check. What's the problem?" I had no answer that wouldn't have sounded like a lecture, a sermon, or a parent trying to "win" an argument, so I let it go.

Before saying anything more, let me add one important piece of information so it won't sound as if I'm finding fault with another teacher and suggesting that he behaved very differently from me. For the first eight years I was in public education, I was a classroom teacher. Just like Kristy's social studies teacher, I gave many assignments which were graded with a check mark or a zero. Anything I might say about him applies equally to me.

## The 'Check-Off'

When we require students to complete homework and then just give it a simple check we are acting in a way that discourages quality. We give students the message that we will accept low-quality work. Kristy, and millions of students like her, learn that almost any work is "good enough" because it's "just homework" and they get credit "because it's done."

Most teachers who evaluate homework like that, and they are the majority, believe strongly in the concept of quality. I would, however, ask those teachers to self-evaluate: Is grading assigned homework that way helping your students do higher quality work? Does our behavior inspire quality?

Most teachers in this situation will tell you that they believe they teach responsibility by assigning homework on a regular basis. Some will even speak with great passion about how they believe it is their role to teach students to act responsibly.

## Grade Deduction

One teacher whom I met at a workshop some years ago sticks out in my mind. He appeared to be dedicated, passionate about his subject, and genuinely liked students—an outstanding teacher in many ways. He was also inflexible when it came to homework. He deducted two points from a student's average at the end of the marking period for each homework assignment which had not been completed. Since he assigned written homework regularly, students typically had twenty to thirty homework grades (check or zero) each quarter. He told me that every year he encountered several students who failed to do homework regularly and who were penalized ten, twenty, or even thirty points each marking period. He was clearly frustrated by this and felt bad when the students failed, but he held firm because he believed he was teaching responsibility. I support his noble intentions. I, too, believe it is important to help students learn to be responsible. I ask this question: Do we really believe that most students who lose points at the end of the marking period learn responsibility? I would suggest that they learn to be resentful, to dislike school, to devalue the subject matter we are trying to help them learn to love.

I came across another teacher when I was conducting a quality school workshop who uses the two point penalty system with her students. She told me that it is not unusual for her to work with students who consistently demonstrate competence on class tests in her math class by earning grades of eighty percent or higher on each test but who receive grades of "C," "D," or even fail because they do not do the assigned homework. "If the students can demonstrate competence on your tests, what difference does it make if they don't complete all the homework?" I asked her. Her answer included references to course requirements, responsibility, and fairness.

Richard Lavoie is the executive director of the Riverview School in the town of Sandwich, Massachusetts, where I live. Some years ago I attended a workshop he gave where he offered this definition of fairness.

*Fairness does not mean that everyone gets the same thing. Fairness means that everyone gets what he or she needs.*

This definition can be particularly helpful when looking at the issue of homework and grading. There are many students, perhaps the majority, who *need* to complete assigned homework in order to learn the required material. There are always some, however, who do not *need* to do each and every assignment or to complete every problem of every assignment. As long as they can demonstrate competence through tests or alternative assessment techniques provided by creative teachers, I believe it is *unfair* to deduct points from their average because they did not complete their homework assignments.

---

***Parents and Homework***  Parents almost always want more homework for their children. In fact, it is not unusual for many parents to perceive those teachers who give the most homework as the "best" teachers in the school. I often wonder if there is more going on in this parental quest for more homework than we may realize. Some parents truly believe that more homework equals a more rigorous curriculum thus a higher quality education. There are, however, parents who want more homework to be assigned for less noble reasons. The more time children are busy working on their homework, the less time parents must interact with them. It is a sad fact, but true, that many parents would prefer to spend as little time as possible interacting with their children. This is not as hard to imagine as it might sound at first. Many children live in single parent homes or in homes where there are two working adults or in families with several children. It is not unusual for parents to have a second job. Many children are very active, inquisitive, and demanding. If children are busy working on their homework, parents get a break. Providing children with a quiet study environment is more culturally acceptable and valued than parking them in front of a TV set. In both cases, the parents get a rest. I'm just not convinced that the agenda is always and exclusively to increase the quality of education.

***Where Do You Stand?*** Take some time and figure out where you stand on the issue of homework. Do the students in your class or classes generally complete the homework you assign? I have met too many teachers over the years who assign homework only to find that a substantial number of students simply don't do it or only do a portion of the assigned work. Compounding the problem is the fact that these teachers begin the next lesson by reviewing the homework that was assigned but not completed. This leads to disruption, a further stratification between "good" and "bad" students, and other problems that make a quality school seem like a distant ideal and unreachable goal.

# TESTS

I don't think I've ever encountered a teacher who did not give tests, unless it was in college, more likely in graduate school. As I write that, I am struck by this thought: We expect the highest quality work to be done in graduate school, especially when it gets to the doctoral level. Is it coincidence that this is the place where we are least likely to find tests and more likely to encounter alternative forms of assessment which ask the student to demonstrate skill, competence, mastery, creativity, and usability? Conversely, on the precollege level we almost never encounter classes without traditional "tests" and we do not get the kind of quality work we desire from students in large enough numbers.

If tests are going to be given—and I accept that they will continue to be given—then it would be wise to figure out what kinds of tests are appropriate and consistent with our goal of teaching. Generally, all tests should lead to the same place:

- What did you learn?

- Why is it important?

- How can you use this knowledge in your life?

Many of us devise tests which focus on the first part: let me know what you have learned. We are far less likely to ask students why the knowledge is important and how they can use it in their lives. If you as a teacher have a hard time determining why the knowledge is important and how it can be useful to your students, you may want to ask yourself why you are bothering to teach it in the first place. What harm can come of that? Teachers complain frequently about having too much material to cover. If you discover that you are teaching something whose importance and utility even *you* can't identify, it may not be worth teaching. Give your valuable time and energy to what you know is important and usable. Interestingly, when you intentionally confront and discover exactly *why* your material has importance and usability, you will naturally become a more energized, passionate, committed teacher because now you *really know* that you are teaching something of value.

### A Learning Opportunity

Tests should be learning opportunities. I stress this continually with my own children. Like most children, they are happier when they earn good test grades and disappointed when they don't. Although I, too, would prefer they experienced more success than failure, I try to avoid that issue and ask them to figure out what they can *learn* from the test experience. Essentially, if students learn from the test it can be a valuable experience. If students do not learn *from the test itself* and tests only serve as a way to evaluate, I believe they are mostly a waste of time. Our goal is to teach and we shouldn't waste time evaluating if it does not simultaneously help us teach. Too many tests are exclusively evaluations and do nothing to add to what students know. If we define schools as places where students learn, then these types of tests are anti-educational. At best they are luxury we can't afford—our time is too precious.

If a test provides students with an opportunity to learn, it is worthwhile. In my mind, the form of the test is less important than the outcome. Multiple choice tests are a favorite target of many educators involved in the quality school movement. Dr. Glasser himself speaks critically about multiple choice tests. Used correctly, however, multiple choice tests can be among the most valuable and educational of tests. My wife recently returned to school and earned a degree in nursing. Most of her tests were multiple choice tests. She and I had some lengthy conversations after some of her tests where she would discuss why several answers were possibly "the best choice." Unfortunately, that learning was not recognized by her instructors. They were only interested in whether she had bubbled in the "best possible answer in the space provided." They never considered using a multiple choice test as a way to have rich, deep conversation that uncovers what is known and what still needs to be learned. As a result, they wound up with information that only allowed them to grade her, not teach her any better. Like many of her colleagues, my wife graduated with honors and passed her national licensing exam, but still wishes she had been taught more and evaluated less.

■ THE TEST AS ASSESSMENT  Even if I wish tests were always structured to teach, I realize that they will continue to be used by many primarily as evaluative instruments. In that case, I hope more and more teachers follow the example of an elementary teacher I had the chance to work with from the Edmonds School District in Edmonds, Washington. A skilled and experienced teacher, she knows that even the second graders she works with can be frightened by "tests." To combat this she has eliminated all "tests" from her classroom. Instead, she and her students have "learning celebrations" only when both she and the students believe the material has been mastered. When I asked her when she evaluates the students she said, "When they are ready to be successful. What would be the point in doing it before then?" After more than thirty years of teaching and observing her students, she knows when they are ready to participate in a "learning celebration." While I have spoken negatively about tests as assessment, this teacher has told me she firmly believes that students need and want the "learning celebrations" because they formally mark and recognize their achievement. Because she uses them sparingly, judiciously, and the experience facilitates the environment by helping students put working hard and learning in their quality worlds, I support this type of testing, even if it is primarily assessment.

■ **THE OPEN BOOK APPROACH** In a quality school, virtually all tests would be open-book, open-note, open-anything you can bring in and use. The questions, however, would be far more challenging and the identification of isolated facts would be of little help. Instead, students would be asked to demonstrate their understanding of the information and its impact on our world today. In this situation, students are encouraged to use all resources, just as you do naturally whenever you have an important problem to solve or decision to make. All you can ever get from those outside sources is information. It is still *your responsibility* to decide how you will act to best satisfy your needs. The same is true of students taking a test. All they can get from friends, neighbors, parents, and other outside resources is information. They still must decide how to use that information as they answer the question.

■ **TESTING WITHOUT TIMING** Timed tests are currently the norm in most schools. While there may be instances when timed tests are consistent with our mission as teachers, there would be few timed tests in most quality schools. Instead, students would be allowed and encouraged to take tests home and work on them. Teachers who rely on memorization of facts will have the most difficulty with this idea, afraid that students will cheat by either looking up the answers or getting answers from their friends, neighbors, or parents. In a quality school this would not be a problem since there would be few times when students would be asked to memorize facts. The memorization of isolated bits of information is inconsistent with the concept of quality work. Research has shown time and again that isolated facts memorized for the purpose of passing a test are generally soon forgotten. Even if remembered, there is little to suggest that memorizing bits of information is in any way useful.

While theoretically there would not be time limits for most tests in a quality school, many students *do* need guidance. Suggest typical times, expressed as a range, that students would spend answering given questions. In this way students know that a particular question *generally* takes between 30-45 minutes for most students to answer completely and *generally* requires at least two well-written paragraphs. Being given general guidelines, not strict requirements, reassures many students. There may even be times when strict guidelines are consistent with a particular learning objective. When my son was being taught how to condense information, his sixth grade teacher developed very specific requirements about how many words could be used in a summary. This is an example of rigidity that is congruent with the goal of the lesson and consistent with good teaching.

■ **A SECOND CHANCE** In a quality school, the focus is on quality work. For this reason, students would *always* be allowed to take tests over if they want to improve their work. In fact, they would be encouraged to do so. Many teachers currently have grave concerns about allowing students to re-take tests. Even those who allow this practice sometimes refuse to give students the higher of the two grades. Instead, they will average grades or indicate that an original test grade can only be improved a pre-determined amount, i.e.,

10 percent. In that case, if I receive a 60 percent on my initial test, and earn a 95 percent on the re-take, I am given a grade of 70 percent. When I ask teachers from around the country to help me understand that rationale, I am almost always told "that's the way the *real world* operates." That has not been my experience in the *real world* where I live. The book you are reading is (for better or worse) the product of numerous drafts and revisions. The publisher did not say to me, "Well. it's not very good, but we'll publish it anyway because you've revised it three times and it's *good enough*." It was accepted for publication only when it was judged to be of sufficient quality. In the *real world*, if you fail your road test and are denied a driver's license, you can take the exam again. If you pass the second, third, or fourth time, you are granted a driver's license and have all the rights and responsibilities of every other driver. They don't average the two scores. Lawyers often do not pass the bar exam the first time, but once they pass, they are recognized as having demonstrated competence. In short, there are countless examples of the *real world* allowing re-tests and giving the higher grade. The *real world* operates on a mastery-level premise. Schools would do well to adopt the same practice.

■ **THAT FINAL EXAM** Teaching to at least a mastery level introduces another point when it comes to grading and evaluation. For the most part, I am opposed to final exams and I especially dislike courses which put a heavy emphasis on one test when a low grade contradicts all the good work a student has done throughout the course. There are, however, exceptions. Specifically, I believe that in a skills based course, if a student earns an "A" or "B" on the final, cumulative exam, their course grade should be no lower. Everything done up until then has been done to prepare the student to demonstrate competence at the conclusion of the unit or course. Even if the student has failed each quiz during the unit, or each exam during the course, if they demonstrate competence at the conclusion of the unit, the grade should reflect their competence. That, by the way, is how the *real world* works in many professional areas. When my wife finished nursing school, she took an exam to be a registered nurse. That nationally credentialing body didn't care one bit about her transcript, her work habits, her attitude, her letters of recommendation, or her effort. They only were interested in knowing if she had the requisite skills to be a registered nurse. As a consumer, I'm glad that health professionals are subjected to rigorous, competency-based exams and I am not particularly interested in how my doctors, nurses, and other health professionals learned the material *as long as they know their craft now and know it well.*

Many teachers disagree with me. They generally believe that holding students accountable for their errors along the way is helping them become more responsible. If I believed that I would join forces with them, but I don't. I have encountered too many students who have demonstrated competence on a unit exam or final course exam, only to be given lower grades because of poor quiz grades or missing homework. Those students, who have the skills to be our future leaders, generally do not learn to be responsible when they receive the lower grade. They learn to be resentful. They perceive school as a series of hoops and driven by their need for freedom, they choose not to jump through any more hoops. The questions are really simple:

1. Are we satisfied that enough students are doing high-quality work?

2. Are we comfortable that many capable students choose to perform as less-than-competent students?

I advocate change because I am not satisfied and I firmly believe that many of our brightest students are turned-off by the system as it is currently structured.

## Alternative Assessments

If one purpose of a test is for students to demonstrate what they know, a quality school would be open to alternative ways to demonstrate competence. Formal tests represent one way to do that. Many students will continue to choose to demonstrate competence by taking traditional tests. Tests would not disappear in a quality school. Instead, under the heading "Demonstrating Competence" there would be several items to choose from, not simply "Tests." The criteria for any alternative assessment would be simple: through an alternative assessment, you must be able to demonstrate at least as much competence as would be demonstrated through successful completion of the test. Any project, written, creative, oral, multimedia, etc., demonstrating at least as much as the test would be acceptable. Teachers are understandably concerned that students may cheat by having someone else do the work. It is both reasonable and responsible for teachers to ask students to demonstrate that the work they have done is theirs. That's not coercive; that's fair. To do less would be to invite cheating, which poisons the school atmosphere and quickly destroys the quality you are trying to inspire.

## Group Testing

Finally, I want to say a few words about group tests. While I value working in cooperative groups and believe students can and should learn a great deal from each other, I am generally opposed to group tests. If student work must be evaluated, it generally should be evaluated individually. This does not mean students cannot work in groups and complete group projects. Each individual in the group, however, should be able to explain what was done and demonstrate competence based upon what the group has produced. Anything short of that invites a situation in which some members of the group do more than their fair share while others abuse the system.

# GRADING

I've thought about the subject of grading for a long time. As someone who has worked in public education for over 23 years, what I'm about to offer may seem revolutionary. Almost every school I know of grades students. Even schools closely connected to the quality school movement issue grades. These innovative schools develop rigorous standards and help students learn until they have demonstrated mastery or quality. At that time, they are given grades of "A" or "B." Perhaps there is no harm in that.

Still, after giving this considerable thought and struggling with this notion for a number of years, I am now ready to say that I would favor the elimination of grading as we now know it in our schools. If we truly embrace the ideas of choice theory, I don't know how we can continue to issue traditional letter grades.

• Such grades represent the external evaluation that choice theorists claim to repudiate.

• Letter grades do little to inform. Especially in secondary schools where teachers typically provide a number of ways for students to earn "points," letter grades tell almost nothing about what has been learned.

### What's The Purpose

In an effort to really get "back to basics," let's take a look at the purpose of grades. Grading, like all behavior, is purposeful. We don't do it without reason. I am afraid, however, that many of us have forgotten the intent of grading and simply "do the math" and issue the "appropriate" grade.

Grades were originally designed to communicate to students and parents what was learned. In a very limited way, they serve that purpose. For example, let's imagine that a teacher just taught a unit involving the multiplication of two-digit numbers by three-digit numbers. At the end of this mini-unit, the teacher develops a test to assess how well the material has been learned. Each of the twenty problems on this test involve the same mathematical skill. A student gets 75 percent of the problems correct and the teacher issues a grade of "C," representing average, or acceptable, accomplishment. In that limited context, the grade has meaning and some value. As a parent, I know my child demonstrated 75 percent competence on that specific skill.

A report card grade is a whole different story. When my child brings home a "C" on his report card, I have no idea what that means, except in the very amorphous and essentially useless way that my child's performance was "average" or "acceptable." What I don't know is what went in to that "C" being issued. I am not suggesting that the grade is not fair, right, or accurate. I'm simply saying that it communicates very little. If the purpose of grading is to communicate information, we would be better served by adopting a more effective system of reporting. Right now, five students in a given class can earn the same grade and have five very different sets of skills, strengths, weaknesses, and competencies. Instead of informing, grades very often confuse and obscure the truth.

### Alternatives To Grades

There are systems of reporting that provide the information traditional grades don't. I had the pleasure to work with teachers in an elementary school on Long Island, New York, where letter grades have not been given for more than fifteen years. They establish their more informative reporting system long before *The Quality School* was written. When I asked teachers in this school how parents felt about their children receiving no letter grades, they assured me that the parents were supportive. In fact, they said parents would be upset if simple letter grades were issued. I then asked if teachers in the junior high, where traditional letter grades are still issued, complained that incoming students were ill-prepared, if they were "less responsible" because they had not been given letter grades. Again I was assured that the junior and senior high school teachers were quite satisfied that the elementary students were learning what needed to be learned and the elementary teachers were teaching what needed to be taught, all without using a traditional letter-grade system. Teachers in this school *do* correct papers, give tests, and provide students with feedback; they just don't issue letter grades on report cards.

In such a school, how do parents know how well their children are learning? Report cards are issued, but instead of the ambiguous letter grades generally provided, teachers provide a detailed report of what skills students have mastered, as well as those that are still emerging. When teachers believe it is helpful, they will provide a narrative outlining the student's strengths and weaknesses. Parents who receive these report cards have an accurate sense of just what their children know. Finally, in this particular school teachers schedule face-to-face conferences with parents up to four times a year. They tell me that relatively short face-to-face meetings provide an opportunity to give parents considerable detailed information quickly and to answer any questions on the spot. The teachers in this school, with their long-term commitment to providing more meaningful report cards, demonstrate that we *can* change systems when we put our minds to it.

As I think about the report cards my own children have received over the years, the ones most helpful and meaningful to me as a parent are easy to identify. They were provided to my wife and me by the preschool teachers. I remember vividly the last report card conference we had with our younger daughter's preschool teacher. We were given a sheet with numerous skills identified. There was a mark after each skill indicating if Melanie had mastered it, was still working on it, or had yet to address it. The teacher commented as she reviewed the sheet and in a matter of just a few minutes, my wife and I had a crystal-clear picture of what Melanie could do. I immediately compared that to an experience I had just a few weeks before that. My older daughter brought home a report card with a "B" in social studies. Unfortunately, a "B" can be legitimately earned in so many ways I had no idea what she knew.

## What Colleges Really Want

When I make comments like these in a workshop, I frequently meet teachers who tell me that they agree with me, but that the system "just can't change." When I ask why, they tend to suggest that we "need" grades because colleges demand them. For quite a while, I reluctantly agreed with them. Not anymore. As my own daughter prepared college applications and examined college catalogues, we both noticed that more and more colleges are encouraging, if not demanding, that students provide portfolios or other tangible evidence that they are legitimate applicants. Essentially, colleges are saying that they know the grading system traditionally used is of questionable value. An "A" in one school does not mean the same as an "A" in another. How can colleges differentiate among applicants? They used to rely more heavily on SAT scores. Most of the better schools are downplaying the importance of SAT's simply because a person's performance on any one instrument, on one particular day, may not be a valid reflection of the student's true ability. The third major criteria, letters of recommendation, are also of dubious value. Teachers generally write favorable letters. Furthermore, those who write letters of recommendation may have a vested interest in helping as many of "our" students get into the "best" schools. What colleges can look at, however, are samples of work that students provide as part of the application procedure. These are concrete demonstrations of what students are capable of producing and give skilled admissions teams valuable information.

Some specialty schools, like art colleges, have been using the portfolio system for years with great success. I am no longer convinced that colleges demand or even want the traditional transcripts that we provide. What they want and need is specific information which will help them evaluate whether they believe a student can successfully meet the academic challenges their institution offers.

---

### It's Time For A Change

Even if colleges were to want the traditional letter grades we generally use, as a public educator I'm not sure that's my concern. My role is to teach students as much as possible. The time I spend evaluating is time I could better spend instructing. The most courageous teachers I know are early childhood educators. They have the strength to ignore the pressure put upon them from above and behave in ways they think are appropriate. They provide developmentally appropriate instruction and refuse to grade. In such an environment, significant teaching and learning occurs. I suggest we follow the lead provided by our colleagues in early childhood education. If we believe in the principles of choice theory and if we believe that letter grades often do more harm than good, let's stop giving them, regardless of the hue and cry of those above us. We can be satisfied knowing that we have done the right thing and that our behaviors are consistent with our mission. We are teachers. We teach. Those students who want to go on to college have the responsibility to provide those institutions with the evidence that they have the requisite skills to be successful. We will help them provide that evidence, but it will not be in the form of letter grades because letter grades communicate little of importance.

# PROMOTION/RETENTION

The question of grade retention generally disappears when students enter high school. In most systems, once students enter high school, they need to pass specific courses and earn a prescribed number of credits in order to be issued a diploma. For the most part, the question of grade retention is a pre-high school problem. Retention almost never has a positive impact upon a student. Most students who are retained dislike school even more than they did before the retention. Convinced that "I've already covered this stuff," they are typically even less engaged by the curriculum the second time they encounter it. Adding insult to injury, they are more likely to be disruptive in class, making it difficult for the teachers to teach and the other students to learn. I have almost never seen a situation where the retained student "learned his lesson," mended his ways, and discovered that doing quality school work would add quality to his life.

*A Matter of Punishment* Why do we retain students, anyway? Although we may not admit this easily, we almost always retain them for one reason: to punish them. If students are incapable of progressing as far or as quickly as their peers, we provide them support through special education, Title I, or some other remedial program. Most of us would never retain students who simply *cannot* keep pace with their peers. Most recognize the unfairness of such a practice. We retain only those who have ability but don't use it. We hope that if we punish them, they will learn to appreciate the value of the education we are trying so desperately to provide. Those of us who believe in choice theory and quality school principles question the value of punishment. Grade retention, therefore, would be virtually non-existent in a quality school.

Are there ever cases where students would be retained in a quality school? Though rare, it is possible for a student to repeat a year. If the student, teacher, and parent believed it was in the best interest of the student to repeat a year, and if the quality of work could be significantly improved, retention may be a viable option. In such cases, however, it would be critical that the student be an active participant in the decision and *really* believed that retention was valuable. If it is perceived as a punishment, it loses its value.

### A Suggestion For High School

Once a student enters high school, grade retention becomes a moot point. Instead, courses need to be completed. While I would do away with traditional report card grades, I would in no way encourage us to lower standards. Here's my suggestion:

- In high school, each course would have a clearly identified set of outcomes, skills, and competencies developed.

- Students would be expected to demonstrate competence in order to be given credit for the course.

- Transcripts would simply indicate that the course had been completed once they had demonstrated mastery.

- No letter grade would be given.

- The specific skills and competencies required in any course would be published and available to any parent, prospective employer, or college.

- Seeing a course listed on the student's transcript would unambiguously communicate that the student had demonstrated skill at a mastery level.

- Until that level had been attained, the transcript indicates nothing, unlike now, when numerous transcripts are peppered with "D" grades, telling anyone who sees it that the student has done poorly, but somehow has passed the class and been issued credit toward graduation.

While most of my colleagues talking about and writing about quality schools favor giving grades of "B" for mastery and "A" for quality, I disagree. Such a system, while certainly a monumental step forward, still embraces a competitive spirit and supports the notion of external motivation. I think it is less cumbersome to simply indicate a course has been completed when mastery has been demonstrated. Quality is difficult to define and somewhat subjective, anyway. Those students who excel in particular areas will be able to develop portfolios of excellence to show to colleges, employers, or whomever else may be interested.

# GROUPING: HOMOGENEOUS OR HETEROGENEOUS ?

Most teachers tell me they would prefer homogeneous classes. Presenting curriculum to students with similar skill levels has obvious advantages. The challenge of teaching heterogeneous classes has increased in recent years as more and more special needs students are placed in regular education classes, further widening the spectrum of abilities the teacher faces in a given class.

How would the issue of grouping be addressed in a quality school? Like everything else in a quality school, the decision should be filtered through the school's mission statement. For example, a school identified as an institution exclusively concerned with teaching academic skills, might choose to adopt a rigidly homogeneous grouping strategy if they believe that students best learn academic skills when placed with peers who have similar abilities. Other schools, however, could identify themselves more broadly. If I were involved in such a discussion, I would adopt the notion that schools are places where academic skills are taught and learned, but I would suggest a vision that would be more inclusive.

A primary mission of public schools is to prepare students to be productive citizens capable of living harmoniously in a heterogeneous world. Many of us live in heterogeneous communities made up of people with different levels of education and income, different values, cultures and races, various religions and beliefs. Public schools can help children learn how to thrive in a diverse community, but in order to do so they need to provide students with the opportunity to meaningfully interact with students different from themselves. Heterogeneous homeroom periods or physical education classes are helpful, but insufficient. If every major academic classroom is grouped homogeneously students are stratified and are ill-prepared to live effectively in a heterogeneous society. If we identify one of our central missions as helping students develop the necessary skills to live effectively in a multicultural, diverse community then we must offer some heterogeneous classes, including major academic areas.

Some disciplines lend themselves to heterogeneity more easily than others. With that in mind, I would not endorse all heterogeneous groupings. It seems appropriate to have some ability grouping, especially if the groups are flexible and less competent students have a reasonable chance to move into more challenging groups when they develop adequate skills. In my vision of a quality school, there would be both heterogeneous and homogeneous grouping to fulfill our academic and social responsibility to our students.

How we conceptualize the role of a teacher has a lot to do with how strongly we feel about the need for homogeneous grouping. What exactly do we think a teacher *does* in a classroom? If you believe that a teacher is someone who imparts information and your vision is of a teacher-centered classroom, homogeneous grouping probably is very dear to you. The imparter of information can be much more successful when given a group of like-learners with similar abilities.

Some, however, have a different vision of what a teacher *does*. While teachers *do,* in fact, provide information, they also function as facilitators. Teachers provide less formal, structured teaching moments, but many more informal, small-group "coaching" moments. As active learners are engaged in the process of learning, this teacher moves from one area of the room to the next—or is visited by groups and individuals—providing what guidance is necessary as students continually discover, learn, and figure out how to utilize new skills and knowledge. In this vision, homogeneous groups generally offer very little because rigid structure is counterproductive, academically as well as socially.

At this point I invite you to take some time and get a clear vision of what you believe the role of a teacher should be. Discuss your vision with your colleagues and see to what extent you agree or disagree. Finally, ask yourselves how closely your picture of what a teacher should do matches what you *actually do* day-in and day-out in your school. Are your scales in balance?

---

## CO-TEACHING

The movement to have more special needs students returned to regular education classrooms has led to a new trend in many schools: co-teaching. Although the co-teaching model takes many forms, the one I hear about most often involves a regular education teacher and special education teacher working together in the same classroom. As I speak with teachers across the country, their concerns about how to make this model work are remarkably alike. The primary issue: who is in charge and how can two adults work it out when both are used to having power and being in charge?

As I listen to the concerns of both the regular ed and special ed teachers involved in this process, I am most struck by what their comments suggest about their vision of what teachers do. Regardless of what accommodating, soft, and politically correct language they might choose to employ, these teachers are struggling because of how they perceive teaching. Given the perception that a teacher is an *expert* who is the center of a classroom, the presence of another adult is a direct threat to power in *my* classroom. Trying to negotiate this arrangement is difficult when power is looked at from this narrow perspective. If I get power from being *in charge of my classroom,* then any concession diminishes my power and is decidedly unsatisfying. I may be able to tolerate it if I retain *more* power than you, if it is clearly understood by all the students that *I am the real teacher* and you are here to *help me* teach the class. Needless to say, that marginally acceptable arrangement is probably untenable for the teacher cast in the role of diminished leadership. In virtually every case, one teacher or another is being asked to give up behaviors previously used in order to satisfy the universal need for power.

### A Different Perception Of Power

Is there a satisfactory answer or is a co-teaching model doomed to failure if you believe in the principles of choice theory? The model can work successfully if teachers are able to conceptualize power in a different way. This does not suggest that the traditional way to perceive power is wrong, but this offers an alternative way to view the issue. If you look at power more generally as representing competence, the situation becomes remarkably easy.

Power does not have to mean that "I am in charge here." It can mean "I am competent." With that perception, any teacher has legitimate power when he or she behaves in a way that helps students make academic and social progress that would be more difficult without the presence of that teacher. It doesn't make any difference which teacher "leads" the classroom at any particular time. In fact, one teacher can lead the class all the time and both teachers can still legitimately achieve a sense of power if they choose to perceive power differently.

Of course, what has just been offered is based upon the notion that a competent teacher is one who helps students learn more and puts schoolwork into their quality worlds. It is not based upon the notion that a competent teacher is one who is the center of the classroom and imparts knowledge to students.

For a co-teaching model to be successfully worked out, therefore, teachers need to adopt a vision of teacher as facilitator and perceive power in a more general way. Given those two shifts, I have seen co-teaching relationships be need-satisfying for both professionals and educationally beneficial to the students. When those two conditions are not met, the co-teaching model will not work with enough success to warrant the energy it takes on the part of everyone involved.

# CHAPTER 11

# *Discipline/ Management*

I conduct numerous workshops designed to teach choice theory, reality therapy, and quality school concepts. In an attempt to offer training sessions that are valuable and need-satisfying, I generally ask the person who contacts me if there are particular issues I should highlight or if there are certain topics that would be especially relevant to the staff. The topic asked for most often, by a wide margin, is discipline. Even though the teachers may be completely unfamiliar with choice theory, they affirm what Dr. Glasser says in *The Quality School:* that teachers generally know how to teach, but they do not necessarily know how to manage students effectively.

Glasser defines both teaching and managing. Teaching involves providing skills and knowledge, utilizing a variety of techniques, to students *who want to learn*. It has been a long time since I taught English, but I still remember that information contained in a subordinate clause can be essential. In this case, the clause *who want to learn* is the critical piece of information. Many of you reading this passage are working in systems which are more crowded now than in years past. Class size has increased. Still, if I were to tell you that your class size were going to increase by 5, 10, or even 15 students, but that every one of your students wanted to learn what you are trying to teach, nearly every one of you would accept that offer in a heartbeat. That's not to say that class size is an unimportant variable. It does, however, illustrate that the single biggest problem we face today in education is that too many of our students do not want to learn what it is we are trying to teach them.

Think for just a moment about any student you have in class who wants to learn what you are teaching. I am willing to bet that you find that student a joy to have in class. Because the two of you have a shared quality world picture of what should be occurring in your class, you have a partnership that makes the discovery of learning a joyous experience. It doesn't even matter much how competent the student is, some students integrate information more quickly and have the confidence to unleash their creativity easily. Others move more slowly and struggle with each new concept. Regardless, all are a joy when they want to learn what you are trying to teach.

Now think of this for just a minute. Most teachers want smaller classes. Suppose I say to you that your class size could be reduced by 5 or even 10 students, but the students leaving would be those most motivated to learn what you are trying to teach and that your smaller classes would be made up of students least interested in learning what you are trying to teach. The majority of you would probably reject that offer immediately.

As Dr. Glasser states, most teachers know how to teach, at least as he defines teaching. Even when we come across a teacher who has some weaknesses, those weaknesses can be overcome with relative ease if all we are asking the teacher to do is to teach *students who want to learn*. The fact is that the job of a teacher in nearly every public school in North America involves something other than pure teaching. As virtually every teacher will tell you, most classes have a number of students who do not want to learn what is being taught. In a great many schools, the number who fit into this category far outnumbers those who want to learn what the teacher is trying to teach. In addition to being taught, students need to be managed.

# A LEARNING OPPORTUNITY

The classroom teacher is a manager. Most choice theorists identify the manager's job this way: managing involves persuading the workers (students) that working hard and doing what the manager wants will add quality to their lives.

While I generally agree with this vision, I have come to phrase it somewhat differently of late. Maybe the word "persuading" is one with which you are comfortable. My perception, however, is that "persuading" involves some distortion. I guess it sounds too much like I'm a sales person trying to get you to buy my product. As an educator, I am not trying to sell anything. I come to this profession from a place of purity and I passionately believe that it will add quality to your life if you decide to work hard in my classroom. With that orientation, I phrase the manager's job more like this:

> The manager is the person who gives the workers (students) sufficient information so that they can better understand and appreciate that working hard and doing what the manager wants will add quality to their lives. It is an attempt to clarify the perceptions of students by providing them with high quality information. There is no persuasion involved whatsoever.

Once students have been successfully managed, they can be taught with relative ease. Managing students is far from easy. It involves a variety of skills, many which have been outlined elsewhere in this book.

## Involvement

In my mind, the first major issue in successful management concerns involvement. The students need to know that you genuinely care about them if you hope to manage them successfully. Teachers need to clearly communicate the following message to every student: "I am here to help you get more of what you want responsibly. I want you to be successful and I believe that with reasonable effort you can do quality work in this classroom."

## Enthusiasm For The Topic

Another component in managing, especially in schools, involves communicating to the students that you care passionately about what it is that you are trying to teach. Very often young children have very little idea *why* learning about a given topic will enrich them in any way. When we, as role models of excited learners, bring our energy and enthusiasm about the topic into our classrooms, the students can better appreciate that it is really worth working hard to learn as much as possible about this subject.

## Communicating Relevance

A third component of managing in a school setting relates to the topic of relevance. The relevance of much of what we teach is not always apparent to students. Recently, I worked with a student who told me that geography was her least favorite subject. When I asked her why, she told me that she just didn't understand when she was even going to use all the information she was being asked to learn. I was working with this student as part of an assessment team to determine if she required special education services. My testing indicated she has an IQ score in the superior range. I am convinced that she has the cognitive ability to learn whatever the geography teacher is asking. Because she doesn't adequately appreciate how learning this will add quality to her life, however, she chooses to do very little in class.

# DISCIPLINE STRATEGIES

When I am asked to talk about discipline to teachers, it almost always means that they want to hear specific strategies, what to do when there is a disruption in the classroom. While I appreciate the value of successful intervention, I am convinced that prevention is always better than even the most successful intervention strategy.

## Dealing With Disruption

Disruption, like all behavior, is purposeful. All we do in life is behave in ways designed to help us satisfy our basic needs or follow our genetic instructions. As a choice theorist, I believe in the basic goodness of people and that they will choose more responsible behaviors when (a) they are available, and (b) they are need-satisfying. With this information about how and why humans behave, I go about setting up a classroom experience that will be need-satisfying for both my students and me. In a conscious, intentional way, I consider each activity I am going to ask them to do, each task I am going to assign.

- What need or needs do they address?

- If the students do what I ask them to do, will they have reasonable chance to follow their genetic instructions in a way that is responsible and growth-producing?

- Specifically, is my classroom structured in such a way that students are encouraged to follow the instruction to belong, to be connected?

- Do I provide them academic opportunities and challenges that let them grow in competence?

- Is my classroom structured in a way that respects the genetic instruction to make choices?

- Is laughter, playfulness, and active learning valued in my classroom?

If I answer "yes" to these questions, I will have very few disruptions and they will be handled quickly and easily. If that sounds like a pipe-dream then I have not been able to effectively communicate to you the validity of choice theory. You see, if I offer a classroom experience that facilitates the students' attempt to follow their genetic instructions by doing what I ask, there is literally *no good reason to disrupt*. If I cannot answer "yes" to any of the questions posed above, I know where the problem originates. Quite simply, some students have pressing needs that cannot be satisfied by doing what the teacher suggests so they do something else. What they do is always purposeful and represents their best attempt to satisfy an unmet need, but it frequently falls into the category of behaviors generally identified by teachers as "misbehavior." Since dealing with "misbehavior" is almost always time-consuming and energy-depleting, it is easier and more effective for me to structure my classroom so that all students can get what they need by doing what I ask. That's the prevention model, based upon choice theory. While I will offer some thoughts about intervention next, the prevention approach will be more need-satisfying for you as well as the students.

■ **INTERVENTION** No matter how good a teacher you are, there are times when students misbehave. The essential issue in discipline is not how to eliminate discipline problems, since disruption is a part of any system regardless of how successful and need-satisfying it might be. The challenge is how to effectively manage disruption when it does occur so that it will not impact the educational process.

■ **END DISRUPTION QUICKLY** What I am about to outline is a reality therapy approach to managing classroom disruption, based upon a model developed by Dr. Glasser many years ago and called "The Ten Steps of Discipline." While Glasser no longer advocates this model, I believe it still has a place in a school working to inspire quality. The objective is simple: to put an end to the disruption quickly. During this very specific process, there is no attempt to counsel in a traditional sense. At the same time, there is no attempt to punish the student. As a classroom teacher, my goal is clear: to end the disruption so that the classroom can better resemble my quality world picture. This process will only be successful in classes that are generally need-satisfying. If the classes are not places where students believe they can meet their needs, this process will not work. In such cases, however, I would suggest that the problem is not the disruption. Disruption is simply the symptom of a more serious educational problem.

*Try This Exercise* To help this process be useful to you, I would ask those of you who are classroom teachers to think about a student in your class who is disruptive. This process is not helpful or appropriate with students who do little or no quality school work, but are quiet. Those students need to find a way to put doing hard work into their quality world and this process will not get them to that place. It's important that you think of the right kind of student for this situation. Specifically, I would ask you to think about a likeable student who disrupts the class. If you believe that this year you have been given the most difficult student in the school, don't consider that student. If you do, you may end up creating a plan that will be less successful. Just as we need to help our students develop workable plans that have a strong likelihood of being successful, we need to develop plans for ourselves that are likely to be successful. So think of the student you like despite his tendency to be disruptive, the student who you believe can be a successful student if he would just give up the disruption.

Once you have a suitable student in mind, you need to do some reflection. Determine exactly what *you* do when he disrupts the class. Forget him and his behavior for a moment and stay focused on what you do. Do you ignore the behavior? Walk over to where he is sitting? Put his initials on the board? Issue him a "check mark" or "strike"? Threaten to contact his home? Issue a detention? Write an office referral? Anything else? Make an actual list of behaviors you have tried with this student who continues to disrupt.

Once you have the list of behaviors you have tried, you need to ask yourself the reality therapy evaluation question: How well are your strategies working with this particular student? Reality therapy isn't simply a *technique* we use *on* others; it is a process we can utilize to help us figure out more effective ways to behave. The odds are that your behaviors have not been successful enough or you wouldn't still be frustrated by this student and his behavior. If that is true, then you would be wise to develop alternative strategies, at least for this student.

It is important for me to say here that I am in no way suggesting that your strategies are not effective with the majority of students. If the things you typically do with students to manage disruption are effective, then I am in no position to suggest you try anything different.

I am not asking you to consider your management strategies in general, but specifically as they relate to this student. Once you have made the evaluation that what you are doing is not good enough for you *with this student* then you need to figure out a better way to handle the situation. What follows is one suggestion for a better way.

Before *doing* anything else, especially as it relates to disruption, you need to remember the importance of involvement. More than anything else, you must find a way to either maintain the strong involvement you already have with this student or to strengthen the involvement if there is not much between you. This is one of the most difficult things you may do as a teacher and illustrates an important issue about the process of reality therapy.

## More Than Common Sense

Often when I conduct workshops, teachers will come up to me during a break and tell me that they especially like the ideas of reality therapy because they are "just common sense." But reality therapy is not *just* common sense. Never is this more obvious than when you are dealing with disruption. Common sense would suggest that you avoid the disruptive child. In fact, there has been considerable research suggesting that teachers tend to spend less time in areas of the room where disruption is more frequent. Common sense tells us that we should get as far away as possible from sources of discomfort and disruption. Reality therapy, however, is based upon the concept of involvement. When you are dealing with a disruptive student, even when common sense would tell you to avoid him, reality therapy encourages you to strengthen your involvement, to get closer to the disruptive student. As long as you maintain your common sense orientation, you will be stuck in an "us versus them" position and somebody will have to lose. Even if you "win" every time, the cost is significant. By abandoning your common sense and working on building greater involvement with the student, you are moving toward a "we" position, where both parties can get what they want and need, but not at the expense of the other.

## Dealing With Older Students

Over the years, I have worked with students from preschool through high school. I have come to appreciate that professionals in elementary, middle, and high schools all work hard and each have their particular challenges. I would never say that working at any level is easier or more difficult than the others. However, I would say that it is often more of a challenge to strengthen involvement with an older student than it is with elementary students. Younger students, even the disruptive ones, are often still "cute" and it's often easier to stay connected to them as we help them figure out more responsible ways to behave. Older students are more likely to have developed more distasteful behaviors and are more likely to engage in behaviors difficult to tolerate.

I remember my first year teaching. I was teaching ninth grade language arts and was giving my first spelling test. The students worked at tables and Tammy was at a table of four. She was flagrantly cheating during the test, copying from her neighbor's paper. At this point in my career I had not heard of reality therapy. Choice theory had not even been articulated. Still, I had some notion that seeing Tammy cheat was incompatible with my quality world picture of what was supposed to be happening. I was young, inexperienced, and realized that *this* situation had not been covered in any of my education courses, undergraduate or graduate level. I asked Tammy to move her seat, and she asked my why. I didn't want to get into a confrontation with her in front of the class so I simply repeated my request that she move. Tammy then behaved in a way that is far too common and spoke the words that I believe no teacher should ever hear. "Well !*!* you!" she yelled and left the room. With only common sense to help me figure out what to do, I avoided Tammy as much as possible for the remaining 169 days of the school year—once she returned from suspension.

If that same situation were to happen today, I believe I would actively attempt to find a way to become positively involved with Tammy even though I still believe her behavior was uncalled for and inexcusable. Tammy and I were stuck with each other for the school year. As an adolescent, specifically one with a number of problems and not a lot of responsible behaviors in her repertoire, Tammy didn't have the skill, strength, or courage to try to improve our relationship. I believe that being responsible means that I need to take that step. There are, unfortunately, more and more students like Tammy and they are seen in earlier grades each year. If we hope to inspire quality in our schools, we have to do more than meet these students half way. We need to be courageous enough to reach out and build a strong involvement with them so they have some chance to develop into responsible citizens. If we don't take those steps, who will? The risk in not doing so is too great. Becoming involved with disruptive students is essential if we hope to have them learn a better way and ultimately put learning into their quality world.

---

### Asking What, Not Why?

Even if you are the most appropriately role-involved teacher in the world, there will be times when students are disruptive in class. The next time the student begins to disrupt, quickly ask the following question: "What are you doing?" While most of what is suggested in this book is fairly flexible and can be tailored to fit your individual style, this question should be asked using these exact words.

It is especially important *not* to ask "why?" when a student disrupts. While "why?" is a perfectly appropriate question to ask in a number of contexts, misbehavior and classroom disruption is not the time to ask "why?" The answer you will receive would almost never be satisfactory. If the student ever told you why (i.e., "I hit him because he hit me first. You just didn't see him"), it wouldn't change anything. You'd still end up saying something like, "Well, I saw you and hitting is not allowed in this room." If, on the other hand, the student answers the question why with a shrug of the shoulders and a "I don't know," you are still stuck.

"Why?" is simply a question that will get you nowhere in this situation.

"What are you doing?" Remember the goal of this process is to stop the misbehavior. If the student stops the disruption, even if he never overtly indicates what he was doing, you can go back to teaching (your quality world picture). I wish it weren't true, but I have witnessed scenes like the following: teachers have asked a student what they were doing and the student stopped the misbehavior. The teacher then chooses to pursue the issue rather than return to teaching. It has sounded something like this: "No, Jason, I didn't ask you to get back to work. I asked you what you were doing. Some of the other students were too busy doing what they were supposed to and didn't have a chance to see your little game. Why don't you tell all of us exactly what was going on." Keep your objective in mind: teaching. Will you be helped by making a bigger deal out of the situation than you need to? Any action you take beyond what is necessary to maintain appropriate classroom decorum is wasting valuable academic time.

"What are you doing?" It is not only the words, but also the tone of voice and body language that are important here. If the question is asked in a sarcastic or accusing way, it is both punitive and ineffective. I would suggest that you ask the question in a way that suggests a sense of bewilderment, like disruption is such a foreign concept that you're not exactly sure what to make of the situation.

### Falling Back On The Rules

If the disruption continues, simply ask, "Is it against the rules?" All classrooms have rules. In a quality school, it is likely that the students have had a say in making the rules. If I were the teacher, I would try to help my students see the *value* of having some rules. Rather than having students perceive rules as necessary annoyances that we must live with, I want them to appreciate that having certain standards of conduct that help us behave appropriately toward one another are beneficial. With rules accepted into their quality world, students are far less likely to break them and far more likely to accept whatever occurs after the rule has been violated. To make things easier in my classroom, I would have as few rules as possible and I would state them positively. "Be courteous and productive" is a rule I especially like, suggested to me by a welding teacher in New York. It is brief, has both a social and academic component, and is stated in the positive. I can think of no behavior to which I would object which would not be covered by this general classroom rule.

Believe it or not, a certain number of disruptive students will give up the misbehavior once you refer to the classroom rules, especially if those rules were developed jointly and have been put into the students' quality worlds. If the behavior continues, however, you simply say to the student, "Will you stop it now?" Again, if the student stops, even if no verbal answer is given to my question, I simply return to teaching the class.

Notice that as the process goes on, there are more and more opportunities for you to begin to behave in less noble, less professional ways. As you provide numerous chances for this student to make more appropriate behavioral choices and he continues to refuse to cooperate, it will require effort and restraint for you not to resort to punishment. The longer you hold fast, however, the more students will realize that you mean what you say: that you simply want to teach and that you have no interest in punishing them or hurting them. As they begin to trust you more and appreciate that you could have punished at several points along the way, they will respect you more and behave more appropriately in your presence.

---

**Working It Out**

Should the misbehavior continue, you need to say something like this to the student: "We've got to work it out." This is the only part of the process that needs to be explained to the students ahead of time so they'll know what you mean when you say it. Tell them that when you say, "We've got to work it out," it means that they have got to figure out a way to behave reasonably in this class. You don't have a lot of rules, but the few you have you believe are important. Since the student is going to be in your class for the rest of the semester or year, it's imperative that he figure out how to behave reasonably. Since you don't want to waste valuable class time saying all of that each time there is a problem, tell them you are simply going to say, "We've got to work it out."

Do students and teachers need to work things out immediately? Some of you may have different ideas, but I don't think it's particularly important that things be worked out right away. The only thing that needs to happen right away is that the disruption stops. If the student stops misbehaving, there is no need to have a conference right then. In fact, you should wait for several reasons:

1. Your job is to teach and you would rather do that than have a conversation with a disruptive student.

2. Taking time now to talk with this student may help him meet his need for power in a less productive way and he will likely be disruptive again.

3. Many of us are better able to work things out after we've had some time to calm down and we can get a little distance from the presenting problem.

For all these reasons, I would be happy if the student simply stopped the misbehavior and I could get back to teaching. Some time later, once I have had the chance to get the students involved in working independently or in small groups, I would go over to the disruptive student and see if we needed to have a brief conversation. If you follow this process and a student continues to disrupt, it seems appropriate to ask the student to leave the room.

- First, if you have tried everything you know at this point, there is little reason to believe you will be able to teach effectively if the student stays.

- Second, the other students are less able to learn as much as possible if you need to give an inordinate amount of time to a disruptive student.

- Third, consider the disruptive student himself. At this point, it is unlikely that he is in a place where he can easily access more appropriate behaviors. It would probably be in his best interest if he were sent from the room and given an opportunity to "work it out."

---

### The Planning Center

Where does a student go when sent out of the classroom? Many schools now utilize what is typically called a planning center. A planning center is akin to a time-out room but with some specifics that make it quite different. Time-out rooms are time-based and time-driven. A student is typically sent to the time-out room for a specified period of time. When enough time has elapsed, the student returns to class. The planning room, on the other hand, is behavior-based and behavior-driven. A student remains in the planning room until they are ready to "work it out"— to agree to behave in ways conforming to the reasonable expectations developed by teachers in concert with students. Consistent with the principles of choice theory, the planning room is a respectful setting where students retain power because *they* are the ones who determine how long they need to be apart from their peers.

You can see now why I indicated that this process will only work in settings which are generally need-satisfying. Let's say, for example, that my classes are generally places where students are able to follow their genetic instructions by doing what I request as the classroom manager. On a given day, a student disrupts the class. I follow the process outlined here, but for whatever reason the student continues to disrupt. Without anger or a lot of fanfare, I have the student go to the planning center. Depending upon the nature of the disruption and the personality of the particular student in question, he needs some time before he is ready to plan to return to class. Because my classroom is generally a need-satisfying place for him, he is motivated to get back to a place where he can meet his needs responsibly. On the other hand, if my classroom is an unsatisfying environment for this student, he will have little motivation to figure out how to return to class. In fact, unless he is unusual, he will try to stay in the planning center as long as possible. When I discuss planning centers with various schools and they tell me it could never work in their building, I get very concerned and curious about why students would rather be in a planning room than in most of the classes available to them in that particular school.

### Staffing The Planning Center

The adult or adults who staff the planning center-have to be very skilled in order for this area of the building to serve its intended function. Ideally, the planning center should be neutral. It's not a punitive, harsh environment. If it becomes too friendly a place, too many students will end up spending their school year in the planning center. If it is punitive, it is inconsistent with the principles of choice theory and incompatible with a quality school. In a quality school, when a misbehavior occurs, we help students learn a better way. Our mission is to teach, and students who disrupt deserve to be taught more responsible behavior. They don't need to be punished, to learn to fear us, and to reject what schools can offer.

Different schools have developed different models in the planning center. Some schools have one or two staff members manage the center all day. Their role description is specific and demanding. Their job is to help students make plans to "work it out," to get back to class. As with all plan-making, they offer as little help possible but as much as is necessary. Typical planning centers develop written forms, completed by students, which specify exactly what behaviors they will exhibit in order to return to class. In my estimation, too many of these forms concentrate too much energy on "what you did wrong that led to your removal from class." While I agree that students need to be aware of what they did that was against the rules, as little time and energy should be spent here as possible. Instead, energy should be focused on the present and future, the development of appropriate behaviors that will allow the student to return to class successfully.

One of the most important considerations in a planning center is that plans must be acceptable to the teacher who referred the student. It is not enough if the planning center manager accepts the plan. As a matter of fact, the planning center staff needs to make sure that they don't get caught in the middle. They need to remain neutral, only helping students develop plans that are acceptable to the classroom teacher. This position of detachment is difficult to maintain and takes an especially strong person. My own bias is that the job of planning center manager is too demanding for any one or two people to do for an extended period. In my experience, planning center managers who have little or no help burn out quickly and disappear.

A more workable model involves a number of teachers who share the responsibility. No one would be in the role of planning center manager for more than an hour each day. Shorter periods or less frequent shifts are preferable. Of course, once you involve more people in managing any system you encounter other challenges. It is crucial that each staff person in the planning center behaves in a similar way. The planning center should have its own identifiable character regardless of who is managing it. If the planning center feels very different at different times of the day depending upon which staff person is managing it, then something is seriously wrong.

In addition to having the strength of character that center helps them interact appropriately with students sent to the planning center, staff needs certain specific skills in plan-making. Just as importantly, they need to know what individual teachers in the school require in a plan. It does no good to help a student develop a plan only to have it rejected by the classroom teacher. In larger schools, teachers should develop school-wide standards that could be used as a guide by the planning center staff.

---

***It's Time For A Change***     Once a student has developed a plan to return to class, the teacher and student should conference briefly. The purpose of this re-entry conference is not to lecture or berate the student, but to provide closure to the disruption, to look forward, and to articulate what will be done in a positive way. I can't overemphasize how important I believe this re-entry conference to be. It is not enough that the student has made a plan with a planning center staff person. It is important for a positive re-connection to be made with the classroom teacher whose rules were violated in the first place. Tammy and I never had such a conference and we spent the rest of the year uncomfortable with each other. With a brief meeting, we might have at least had a chance to learn how to be more successful with each other.

One last thought about planning centers, especially when used in secondary schools where students move from teacher to teacher. If a student has caused a disruption in an English class, then I believe she should be allowed to leave the planning center at the end of that period and go to the next class provided she poses no threat to herself or anyone in the building. If she has not worked out a plan with the English teacher, she would not report to English the next day, but would return to the planning center. She would, however, be allowed to attend the rest of her classes without any punishment.

There are several reasons why I favor this approach as opposed to the "stay in the planning center until you work it out" approach advocated by some. For one thing, let's pretend this student has math class after English. I have heard of cases where the student has missed a math test because of a problem he had with the English teacher. Because of school policy, the math teacher is required to prepare a separate make-up exam for the student and keep him after school to take it. In this case, the math teacher is now being punished, perhaps because the English teacher has poor management skills. Once one teacher is punished because of the behavior of another, morale begins to suffer and quality is never attainable in such a setting. Another reason to allow the student to go to the next class is to keep him positively connected to school in as many places as possible. Instead of punishing the student, the school essentially tells the student, "We have this problem in English that needs to be worked out and you can't go back to English until you've figured out a way to work it out. In the meantime, we want and expect you to be as successful as you can be in your other classes."

When the student has violated school-wide rules and not just disrupted a particular class the student should remain in the planning center until he has figured a way to "work it out," even when it means missing multiple classes. It is appropriate for the student to be removed from all school activities and classes until he has figured out a better way.

## When Things Aren't Working

How long can a student stay in a planning center? Each school has to figure that out for itself. Certainly, I would offer counseling and assistance to any student who seemed intent on remaining in such a neutral place. Even though work could be completed in the planning center and full credit received, it is more difficult to learn there because the classroom teacher is not there to coach the student. At some point, parents need to be notified that their son or daughter is choosing to spend time in a planning center rather than in class. Before taking such a step, I tell the student that we need to tell parents because they pay our salary and have certain beliefs about what goes on within the school. When things are very different, parents deserve to be informed. Some would accuse me of being coercive by doing this. I disagree. As long as the student has an opportunity to control what happens and my intentions remain pure and non-punitive, I feel comfortable behaving in this way. I am merely providing information to others so they can make informed decisions. Of course, if I deliver that same information in a nasty, sarcastic way, it would quickly erode into a punitive, coercive strategy which would undermine my stated goal of inspiring quality in our schools.

The planning center concept is just one component designed to maintain a positive atmosphere in a quality school. The entire approach to discipline in a quality school is built upon one premise: our job is to teach students more appropriate behavior when they misbehave. Punishment is not even considered. What drives our behavior as teachers is to ask ourselves this question: given this student's choice of behavior, what can *I* do at this point which will help him learn more appropriate, responsible behaviors? Discipline is intimately connected to teaching, and the strategies we choose should be based upon whether or not they are consistent with our mission as educators.

# SOME FINAL THOUGHTS ON DISCIPLINE

At the risk of being redundant, it is critical to remember that only minimal energy and attention should be spent in the area of discipline. To inspire quality in your school, focus your energy on building involvement, developing quality relationships, and helping students see the value of putting academic work into their quality worlds. In such a setting, discipline problems are rare and easily managed.

Each school actively and intentionally striving to inspire increased quality will face its own set of unique challenges. What I have offered here are some thoughts I believe are consistent with the principles of choice theory and may be of some assistance to the majority of schools undertaking this journey. Your particular school may have additional issues to address: dealing effectively with parents; interacting positively with other agencies; using effective behaviors during multidisciplinary team meetings; managing the playground effectively; or managing the cafeteria effectively.

Regardless of what issues you decide to address, the process you use remains the same. Ideas are referred back to your mission statements. Using the principles of choice theory and reality therapy, you collectively develop the most appropriate course of action you can at that time, knowing that you will make additional changes if modification would lead to higher quality. As long as individuals keep the ideas of choice theory in mind as they strive to create better schools and consciously work to respect each other, meaningful gains will be made. In such an atmosphere, change can occur in an exciting and worthwhile way.

# Closing Thoughts

It doesn't seem right to have a *Conclusion* to a book about inspiring quality in your school since quality is an ongoing process and never reaches a conclusion. Still, it would seem unfinished if I didn't provide a few thoughts in closing.

- Theory, by itself, can take us only so far.

- Theory, by itself, is ultimately empty.

- Practice that is not built upon a solid, consistent theory is insufficient.

- Practice that is not built upon a solid, consistent, valid theory is aimless.

*Inspiring Quality in Your School: From Theory to Practice* offers us a chance to develop a repertoire of practices and behaviors that are congruent and consistent with a sound theory about how human beings behave. Evolving educational practices from a well-grounded theory of human behavior gives us an opportunity to inspire the kind of quality we might envision. Teachers, students, and their parents deserve no less. I wish you success as you continue your quest to build an even better school.

# Suggestions for Further Reading

Covey, S. 1989. *The 7 Habits of Highly Effective People*. New York: Simon & Schuster.

Crawford, D., Bodine, R., and Hoglund, R. 1993. *The School for Quality Learning: Managing the School and Classroom the Deming Way*. Illinois: Research Press.

Floyd, C. 1990. *My Quality World Workbook*. North Carolina: New View Publications.

Glasser, W. 1984. *Control Theory*. New York: Harper Collins.

——— 1986. *Control Theory in the Classroom*. New York: Harper Collins.

——— 1990. *The Quality School: Managing Students Without Coercion*. New York: Harper Collins.

——— 1993. *The Quality School Teacher*. New York: Harper Collins.

Gossen, D. and Anderson, J. 1994. *Creating the Conditions: Leadership for Quality Schools*. North Carolina: New View Publications.

Greene, B. 1994. *New Paradigms for Creating Quality Schools*. North Carolina: New View Publications.

Jensen, E. 1995. *Brain-Based Learning & Teaching.* California: Turning Point Publishing.

Kohn, A. 1993. *Punished by Rewards: The Trouble With Gold Stars, Incentive Plans, A's, Praise, and Other Bribes.* Boston: Houghton Mifflin Company.

Sullo, R. 1993. *Teach Them To Be Happy.* North Carolina: New View Publications.

Tinsley, M. and Perdue, M. 1994. *The Journey to Quality.* North Carolina: New View Publications.

Watson, J.B. 1930. Behaviorism (rev. ed.). Chicago: University of Chicago Press. (Originally published 1925).

## ACKNOWLEDGEMENTS

There are so many people who have helped me along the way that it is impossible to acknowledge them all. I first want to thank the hundreds of teachers who have taken time during workshops to share their stories, their frustrations, and their successes. I have tried to include your collective wisdom in the following pages. Dr. William Glasser continues to teach, challenge, and encourage me as I try to help schools move towards increased quality. Nora Todd, consultant for the Massachusetts Teachers Association Division of Professional Development, and Roseanne Bacon, past president of the Massachusetts Teachers Association, were particularly helpful to me as I sought the right audience for my ideas. Timothy Crawford and Lisa Kenefick of the NEA Professional Library have made the task of publishing a true pleasure. I want to acknowledge several people in the Plymouth Public Schools, where I have worked for the past 23 years. Dean Koulouris, Director of Pupil Personnel Services has continually supported my professional growth and development in a manner which deserves special thanks. Bernard Sidman, Superintendent of Schools, and Paul Vecchi, Assistant Superintendent of Schools, have given me the opportunity to reach out to other districts while continuing to serve the students of Plymouth, Massachusetts. Finally, I am forever grateful to my wife Laurie and our children Kristy, Greg, and Melanie who provide me with the love and support I value more than everything else. To all of these people and others too numerous to name, I thank you very much.

**Robert Sullo** is a school psychologist with Plymouth Public Schools in Massachusetts. He has been involved in public education since 1974. As a senior faculty member with The William Glasser Institute, he travels across the country conducting professional development seminars and workshops promoting choice theory and reality therapy

If you are interested in workshops, presentations, or other speaking engagements by the author, please contact Bob Sullo directly at:

PO Box 1336
Sandwich, MA 02563
tel: (508) 888–7627
e-mail: rasullo@capecod.net

For additional information, visit the author's website: http://www.capecod.net/bobsullo